I0824058

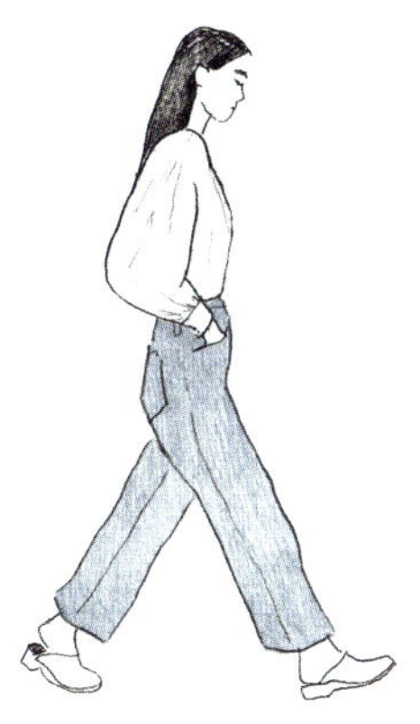

Alessandra Olanow

BEGIN AGAIN AND AGAIN AND AGAIN

Notes on the art of perpetual renewal

Workman Publishing
New York

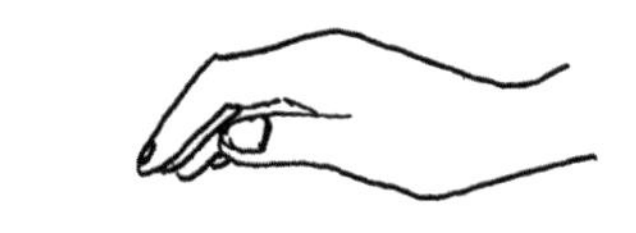

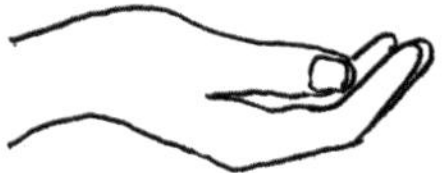

MAY I BE SAFE
MAY I BE HAPPY
MAY I BE HEALTHY
MAY I LIVE WITH EASE

MAY YOU BE SAFE
MAY YOU BE HAPPY
MAY YOU BE HEALTHY
MAY YOU LIVE WITH EASE

May we allow ourselves to
start over, trust the unfolding,
find beauty in the beginning.

—Adapted from the Buddhist loving-kindness meditation

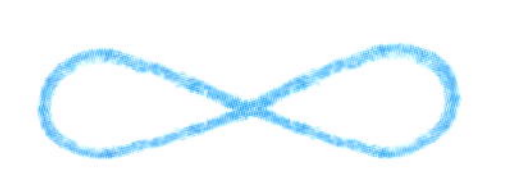

CONTENTS

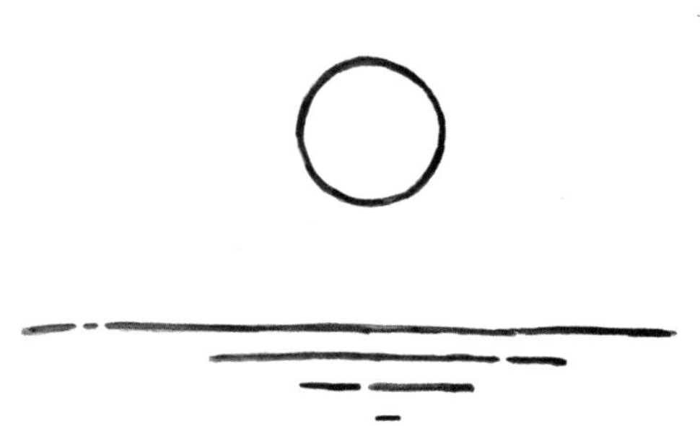

INTRODUCTION

In 2020, I wrote *I Used to Have a Plan*; I drew my way through divorce, loss, and change, learning to embrace the messiness of life. At the time, I thought that was the hard part.

The harder part, it turns out, is what comes after. When life unravels again—as it inevitably will. When what we've carefully built comes undone—as it somehow always does. The beginning again. And again. And again.

This book started as notes to myself at 3 a.m., when the city was quiet and my daughter was asleep. When the questions would rise like the tide: *Is this all there is? Am I doing it right? What comes next?* I found myself drawing again, but this time not just to cope. To understand. To map the territory of starting over. To trace the shape of transformation.

What I've learned is that transformation isn't a single moment of breakthrough. It's a continuous cycle of breaking open, of questioning, of finding ground, of beginning again. This book is for anyone who has ever stood in their carefully built life and felt something stirring. For those wondering if there's more. For those ready to begin again.

Because the truth is, we're all just practicing. Always just beginning. Over and over and over.

To everyone who is rebuilding, whether by choice or by circumstance: May these pages be a reminder that it's never too late to begin again.

With love,

ALESSANDRA

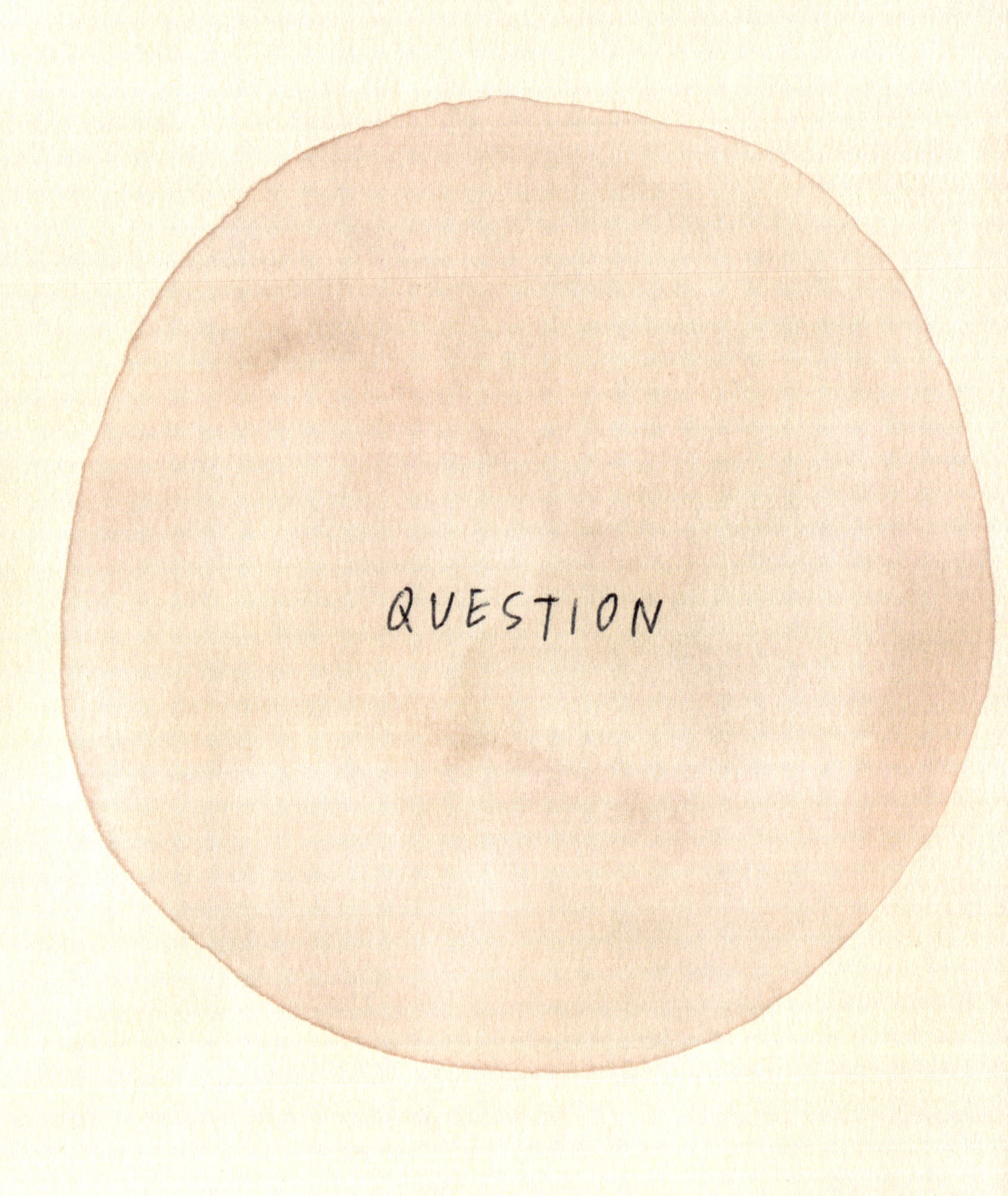
QUESTION

PART 01: IS THIS ALL THERE IS?

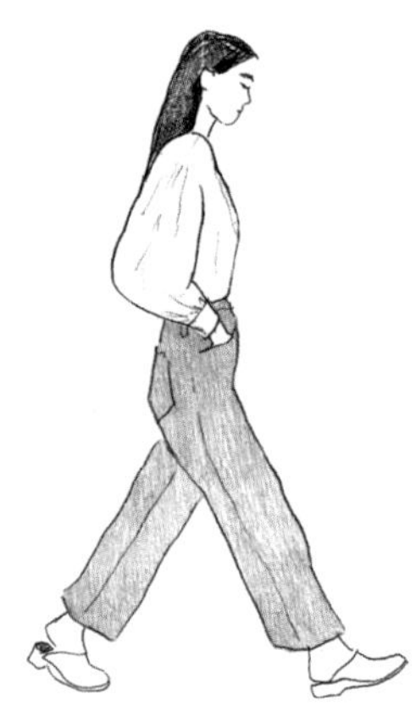

QUESTION

The question, *is this all there is?*, arrived uninvited, the way important things often do—slipping in during those quiet moments when defenses are down. I was forty-four, lying in a bed I'd chosen, in a life I'd built, wondering why it felt like I was wearing someone else's clothes.

From the outside, my life looked settled. Inside, something felt hollow. I'd spent years chasing the next thing—the relationship that would complete me, the achievement that would prove my worth, the experience that would finally make me feel alive. Instead, I found myself tired from all that reaching, weighed down by the nagging sense that I'd missed something essential along the way.

What I didn't know then was that this question would return again and again, each time asking me to shed another layer of who I thought I should be.

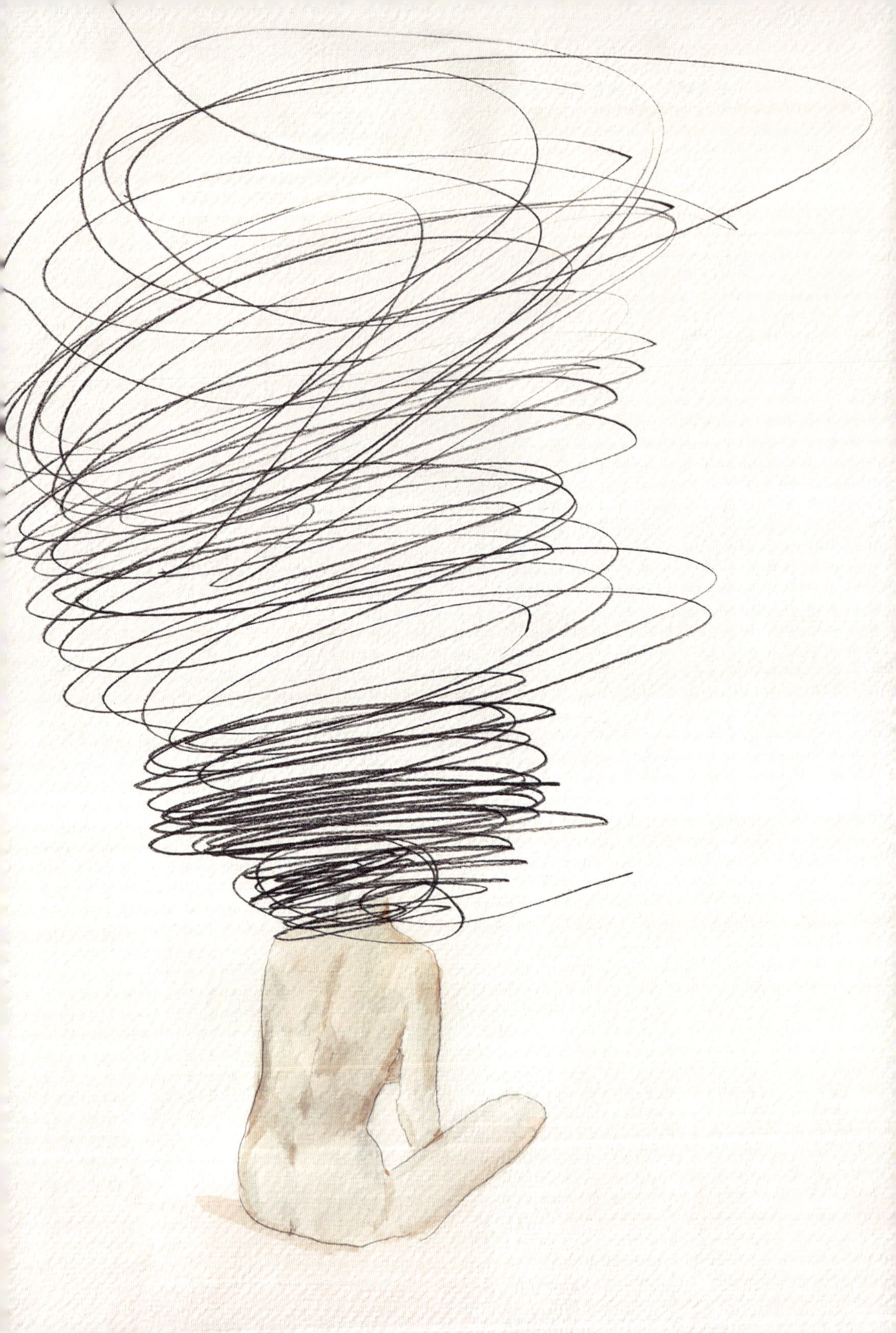

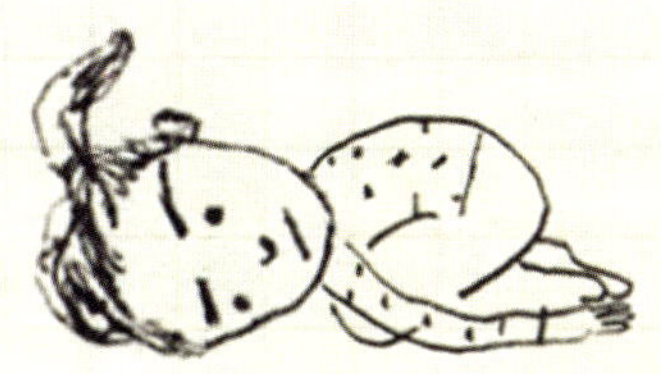

YOUR BODY HEARS EVERYTHING
YOUR MIND SAYS.

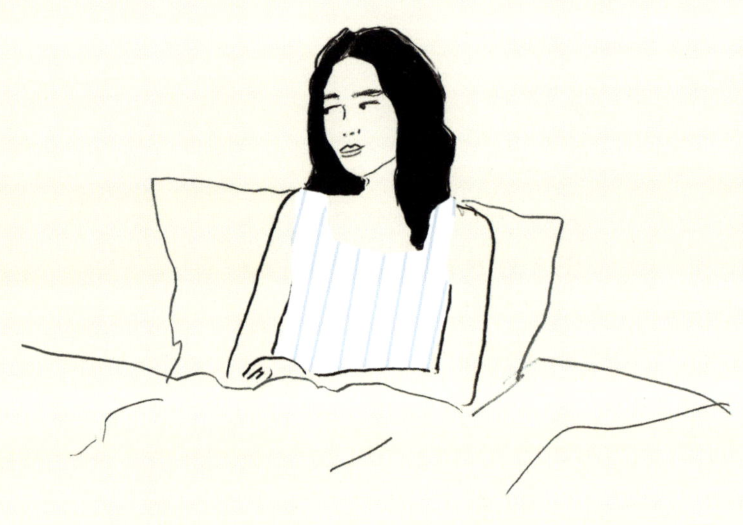

IT'S 3A.M. SOMETHING HOLLOW HAS SETTLED INSIDE ME, AND TONIGHT IT FEELS HEAVY. I LIE HERE TAKING INVENTORY. THE WAYS I'VE MADE MYSELF SMALLER. THE CAREFUL ACCOMMODATIONS THAT SEEMED HARMLESS AT THE TIME. EACH ONE A THREAD IN A FABRIC THAT NO LONGER FITS. THE QUESTIONS SETTLE QUIETLY BETWEEN MY RIBS.

WHEN DID THIS HAPPEN? WHEN DID I BEGIN PERFORMING MY OWN LIFE?

I CAN FEEL WHERE THE SEAMS PRESS WRONG, WHERE I'VE BEEN SEWN INTO SOMEONE ELSE'S PATTERN.

THE RECOGNITION IS NOT RELIEF.

IT'S 3A.M. AND I UNDERSTAND SOMETHING I COULDN'T YESTERDAY. THERE IS NO UNKNOWING THE WEIGHT OF WEARING SOMEONE ELSE'S LIFE.

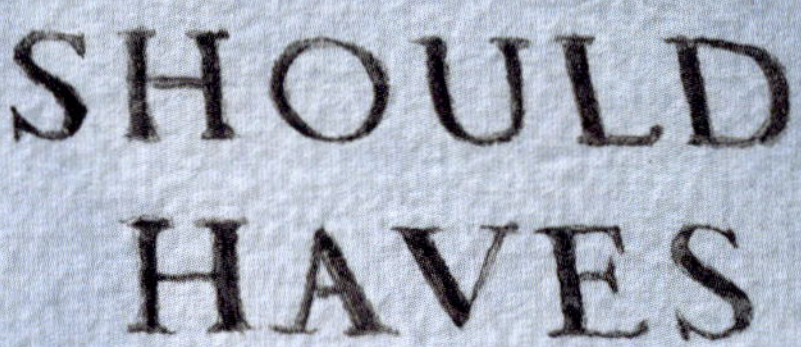
SHOULD
HAVES
STORIES OF ALMOST
VOL.01

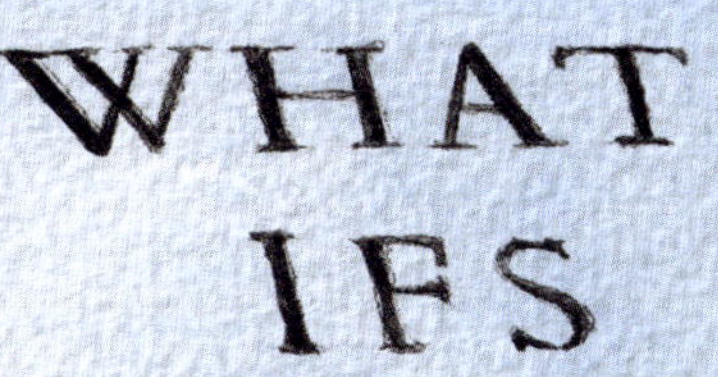
WHAT
IFS
TALES OF NOT QUITE
VOL.02

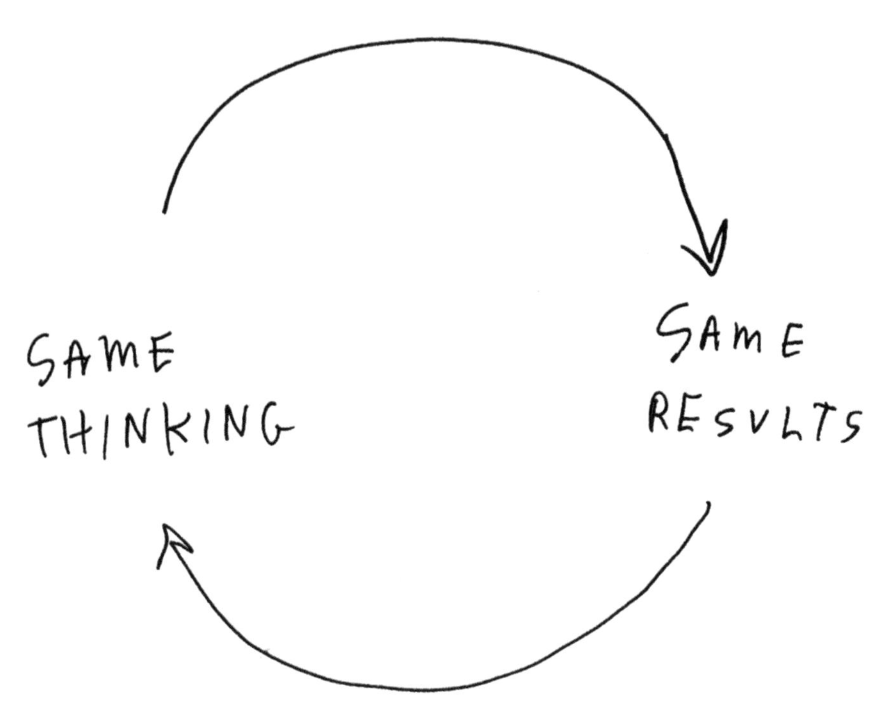
SAME THINKING
SAME RESULTS

LIFE IS NOT
HAPPENING
TO YOU.

IT'S RESPONDING
TO YOU.

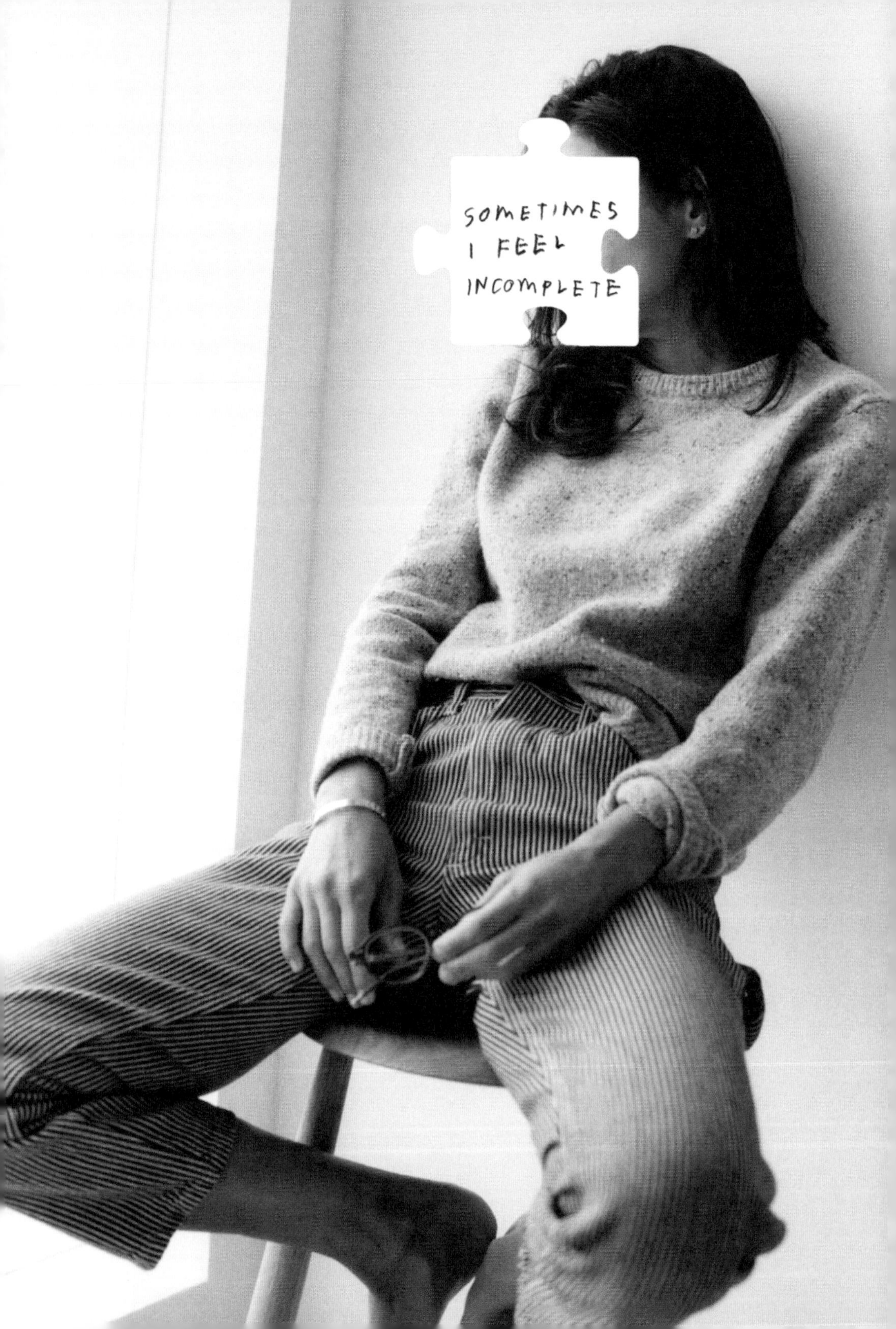
SOMETIMES
I FEEL
INCOMPLETE

In the mirror, I am a collection of unfinished sentences, a book with pages torn out. My reflection speaks in ellipses, trailing off. . . I am learning to love the spaces between words, the silence between heartbeats. There is beauty in the uncarved stone and we are all works in progress.

Listen; in the quiet moments, you can hear the universe expanding. We too are expanding, reaching for something just beyond our grasp. This incompleteness is not emptiness but room for wonder. We are unfinished symphonies. Maybe our most beautiful notes are yet to be played. So I celebrate the draft, the sketch, the wondering. I ask myself, is being incomplete what makes us whole?

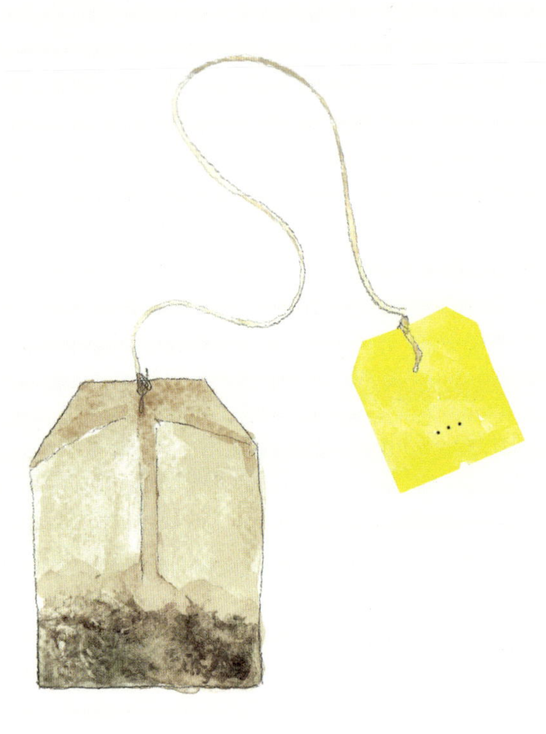

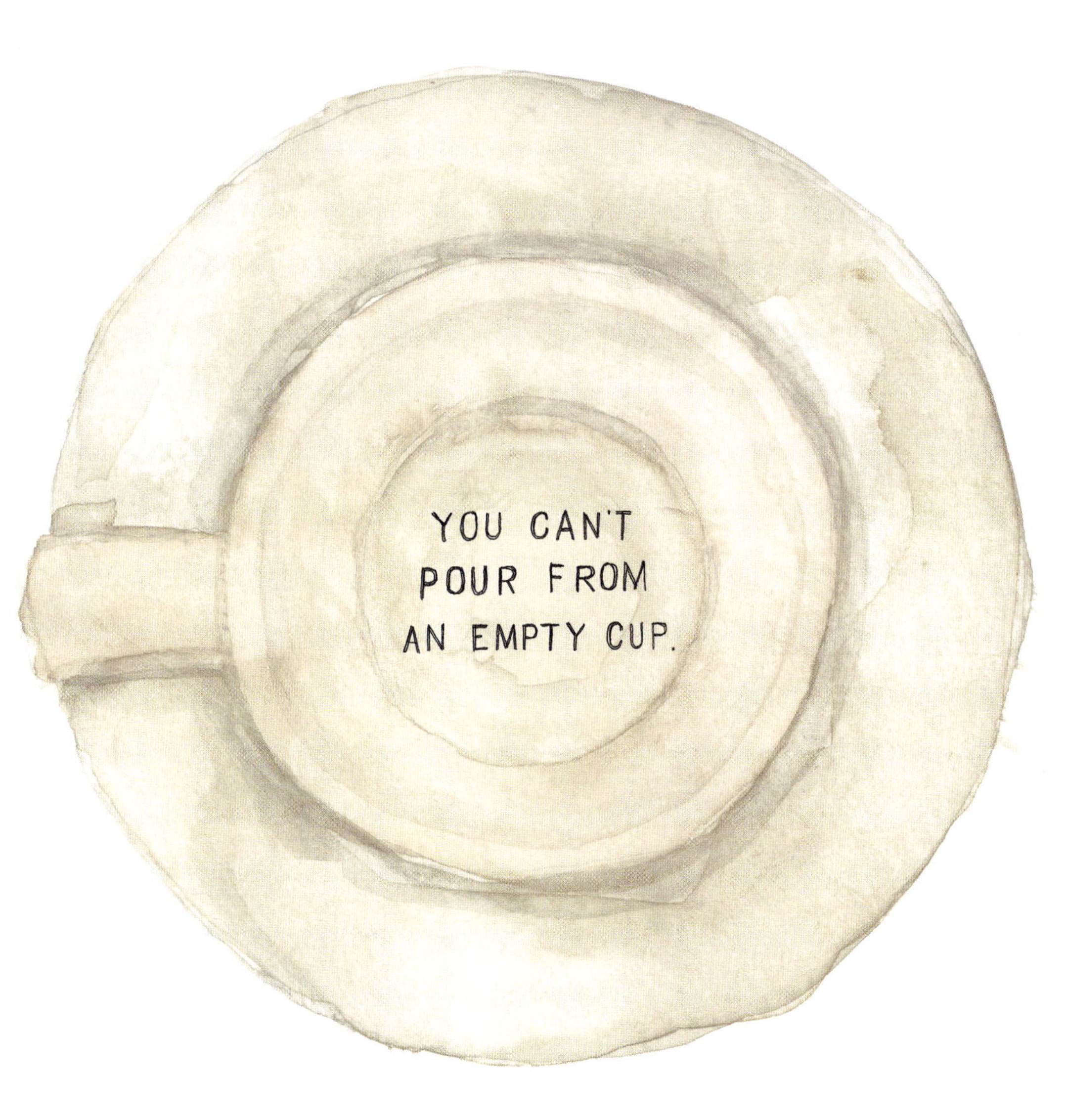
YOU CAN'T
POUR FROM
AN EMPTY CUP.

TRYING TO CONTROL
WHAT IS OUTSIDE
YOUR CONTROL
WILL CONTROL YOU.

Inside my control
Are my opinions,
Attitudes, hopes, desires,
How I spend my free time,
What books I read,
What I eat, what I drink,
Who I spend time with.

Outside my control
Is everything else...
The family and body I was born into,
The weather, the state of the world,
What other people think about me,
How life's events unfold.

I'm working on what I can control:
My perception of a situation,
How I react to it,
And what actions I can take in response.

WHERE WE FOCUS DETERMINES WHAT WE FIND

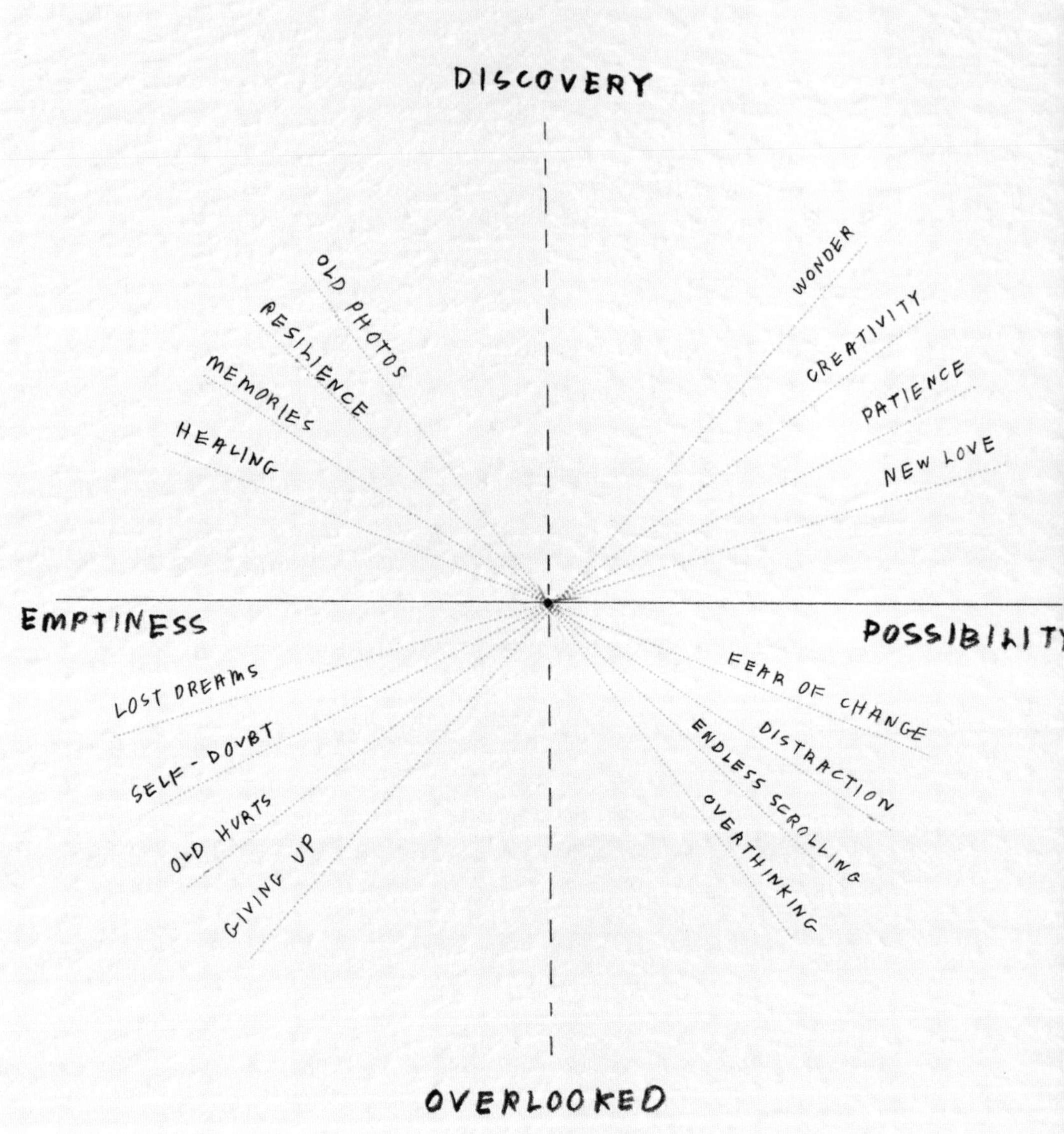

WHAT WE SEE
DEPENDS ON
WHAT WE
LOOK FOR

LIGHTLY CHILD,
LIGHTLY

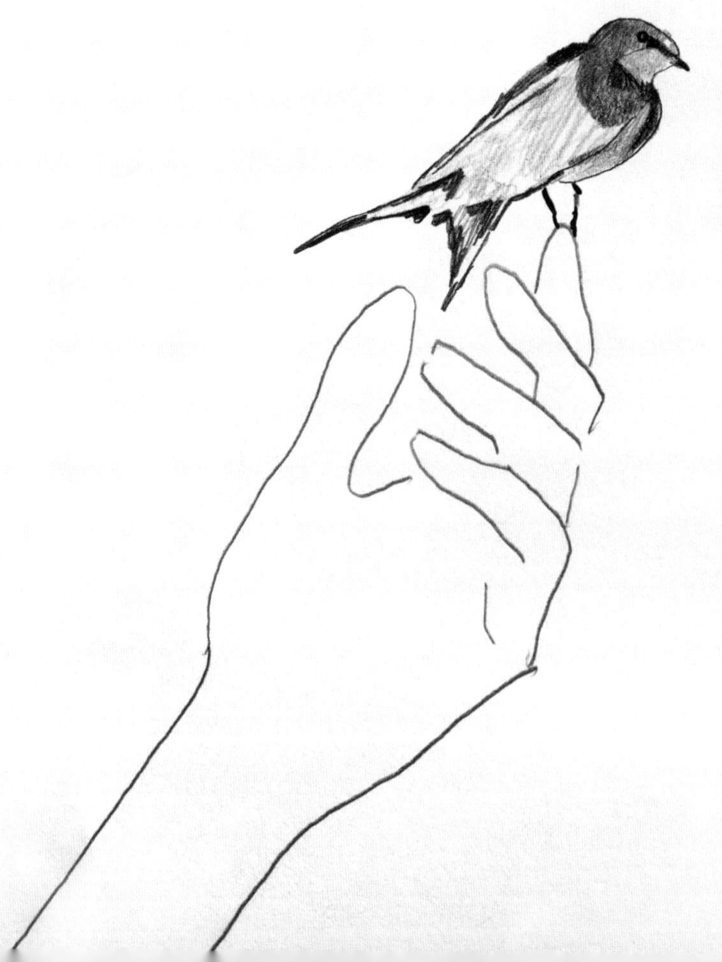

A child notices a sparrow. Before the word *sparrow* forms, there's pure attention—complete, alive, asking nothing.

We've lost this way of seeing. We name everything, sort it all into categories. Each label becomes a small weight we carry, shaping what we notice next.

What if we could see fresh again? As Aldous Huxley said, "lightly child, lightly"—hold our knowing more gently. In that pause between seeing and naming, something alive waits.

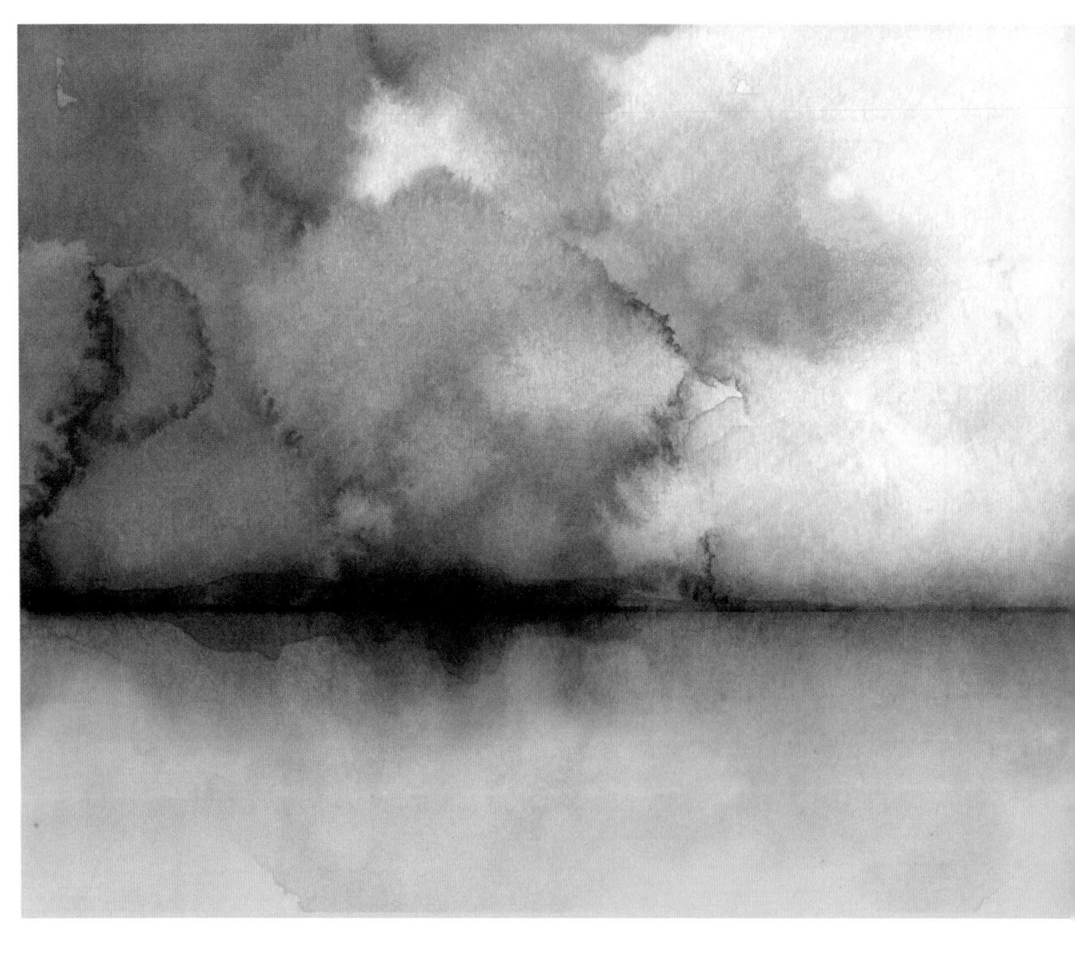

PERHAPS THE QUESTION
IS NOT WHAT MORE,
BUT WHAT DEEPER
AWAITS YOU.

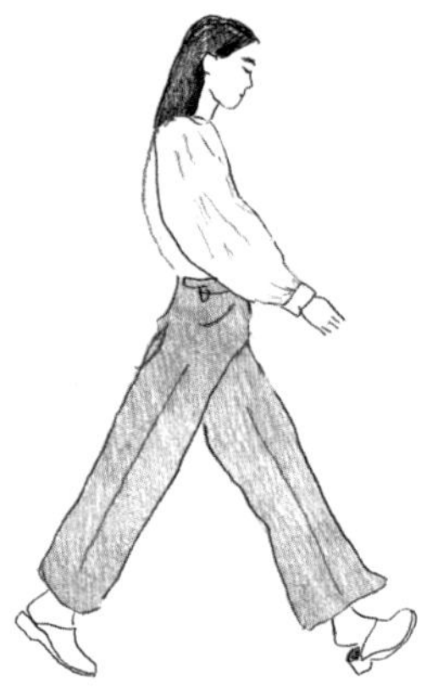

BEYOND THE QUESTION

Buddhism speaks of dukkha—the unsatisfactory nature of ordinary existence. The question "Is this all there is?" is dukkha manifesting, inviting us to look deeper. And in time, I did.

What I discovered wasn't a destination but an opening. The practice of sitting with the present moment revealed that "all there is" constantly shifts and changes. Every time I thought I'd found the answer, life would move again, presenting new possibilities to explore.

This recognition—that we are never truly finished becoming—is tender territory. The beauty lies not in arriving at some perfect understanding but in the continuous cycle of questioning and discovery. When I stopped demanding that life reveal all its mysteries at once, I could finally participate in its gradual unveiling.

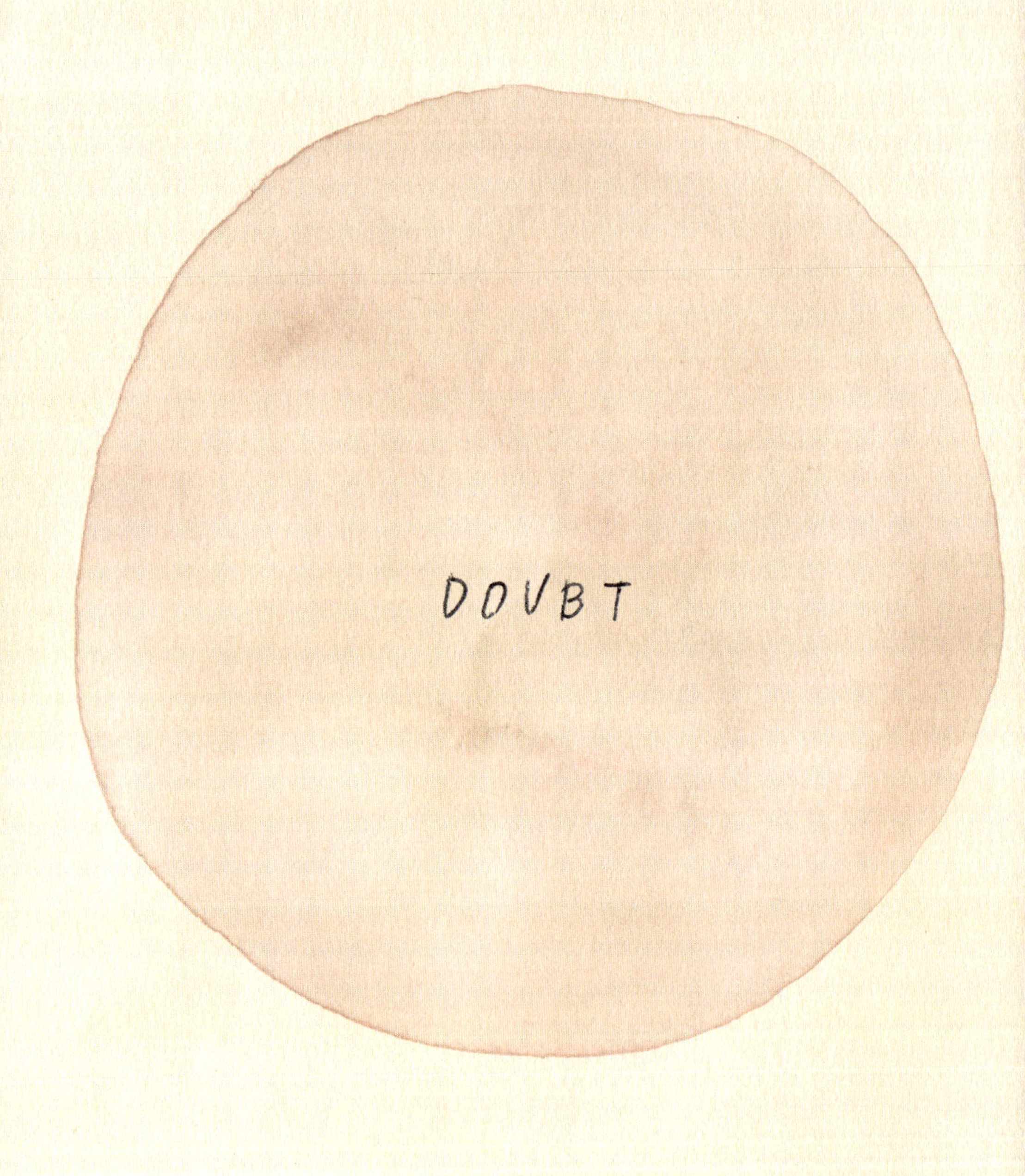
DOUBT

PART 02: I THINK I CAN'T

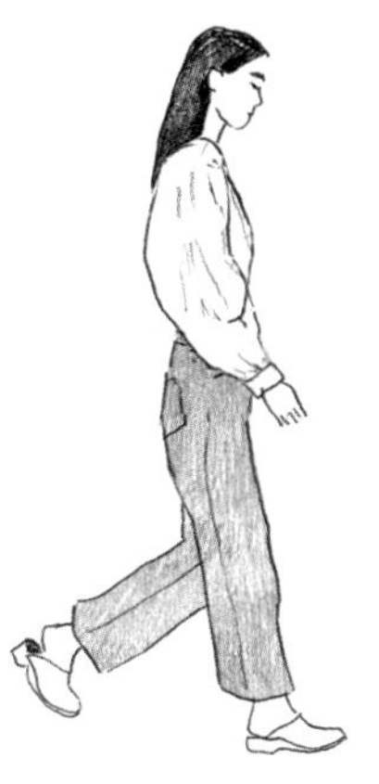

DOUBT

"I think I can't" became my silent mantra somewhere along the way. Not the dramatic kind of self-doubt that announces itself, but the everyday kind that whispers from the corners—too old, too late, not that kind of person.

This self-doubt is born from the wounds of our past, etched into our psyche by moments of failure, criticism, or comparison. It's a shadow cast by the expectations of others and the fear of not measuring up. What begins as a fleeting thought in youth calcifies over time, becoming a lens through which we view our capabilities and potential.

These weren't conscious thoughts so much as background music, the soundtrack to a life lived within careful boundaries. I wore these limitations like old sweaters—familiar, comfortable, put on so automatically that they became invisible to me, until someone asked why I was still wearing wool in July.

YOUR THOUGHTS DON'T DEFINE YOUR REALITY.

REMEMBER THIS
WHEN DOUBT APPEARS,
JUST BREATHE
AND SEE CLEARLY.

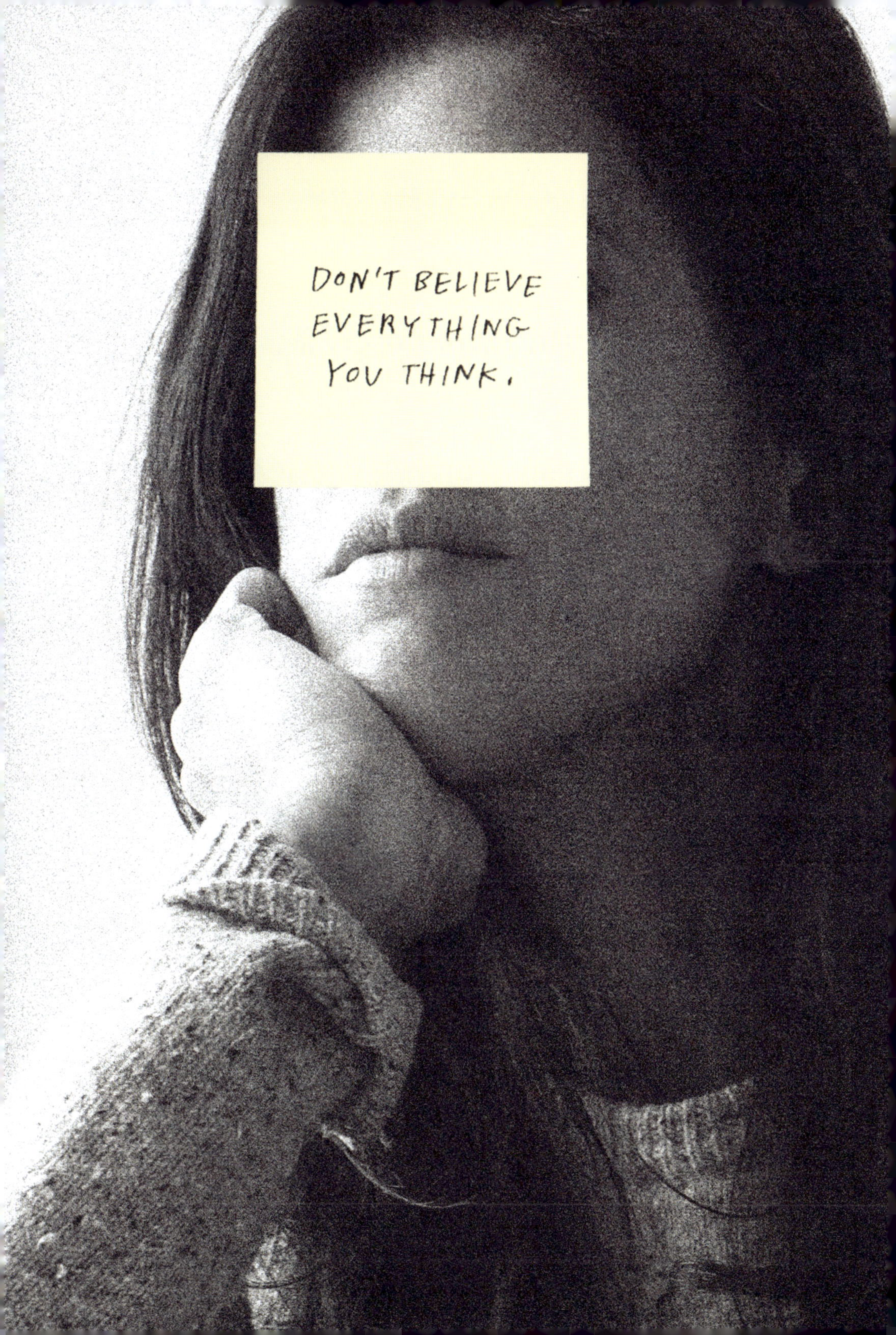
DON'T BELIEVE
EVERYTHING
YOU THINK.

BUBBLE
WRAP

We outgrow not just clothes
but thoughts, habits, relationships, and fears
that once fit snugly around our hearts.

It can feel uncomfortable
this stretching beyond old boundaries
but discomfort is often
the first sign of expansion.

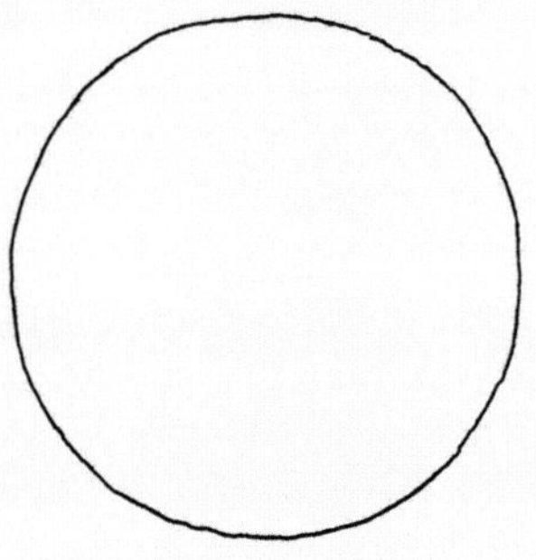

WHEN I'M SCARED

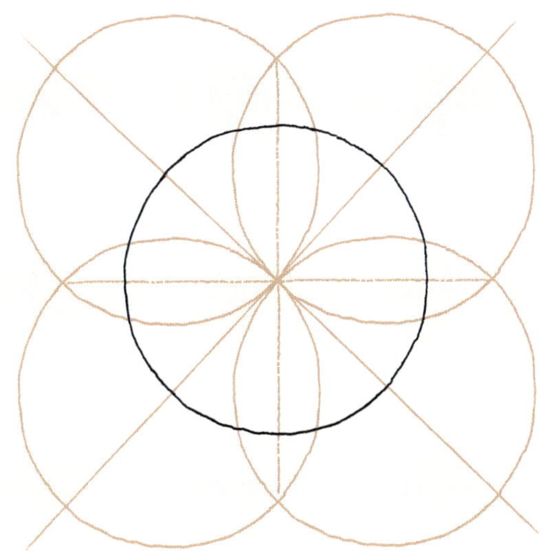

WHEN I TRUST

TO DO:

- ☐ RENEW DRIVER'S LICENSE
- ☐ FIX SHELF IN CLOSET
- ☐ CALL EDWARD
- ☐ ASK THERAPIST IF DRAWING MYSELF ALL THE TIME MAKES ME A NARCISSIST
- ☐ GET COCO NEW SNEAKERS
- ☐ BE YOURSELF
- ☐ FIGURE OUT WHAT "YOURSELF" REALLY MEANS
- ☐ ORDER MORE COFFEE FILTERS
- ☐ MEDITATE
- ☐ FIGURE OUT WHY I KEEP CLOTHES THAT HURT MY FEELINGS
- ☐ ACHIEVE ENLIGHTENMENT THROUGH LAUNDRY-FOLDING
- ☐ SCHEDULE PHYSICAL
- ☐ COCO DENTIST
- ☐ MAMMOGRAM
- ☐ SET UP NEW BANK ACCOUNT
- ☐ CALL ACCOUNTANT
- ☐ NEW TIRES / CAR
- ☐ STOP STARTING EVERY OTHER SENTENCE WITH "I'M SORRY"
- ☐ MEET WITH TIM TO REVIEW CO-PARENT SCHEDULE
- ☐ PONDER WHETHER DISHES IN THE SINK EXIST WHEN NO ONE IS LOOKING
- ☐ DEAL WITH E.R. MEDICAL
- ☐ HAIRCUT
- ☐ CANADIAN PASSPORT
- ☐ ANNUAL SKIN CHECK
- ☐ MORNING PAGES
- ☐ TRAIN FOR UPCOMING MARATHON (OF NETFLIX EPISODES)
- ☐ DO NOTHING
- ☐ ORDER PRINTER PAPER / INK
- ☐ CLEAR OUT INBOX
- ☐ DEBATE WHETHER THINKING ABOUT EXERCISE COUNTS AS MENTAL FITNESS
- ☐ REINVENT MYSELF AGAIN

WHEN YOU DON'T KNOW
WHERE TO BEGIN
WITH YOUR LIST OF
31 THINGS THAT
NEED TO GET DONE.

REMEMBER
THAT IT'S OKAY
IF YOU HAVE TO GO A
LITTLE SLOWER THIS
PARTICULAR DAY.

YOU ARE
ALLOWED TO TAKE
A LITTLE MORE
TIME.

SOMETIMES

THE FUTURE IS UNCLEAR

AND WE HAVE TO GO

FORWARD ANYWAY

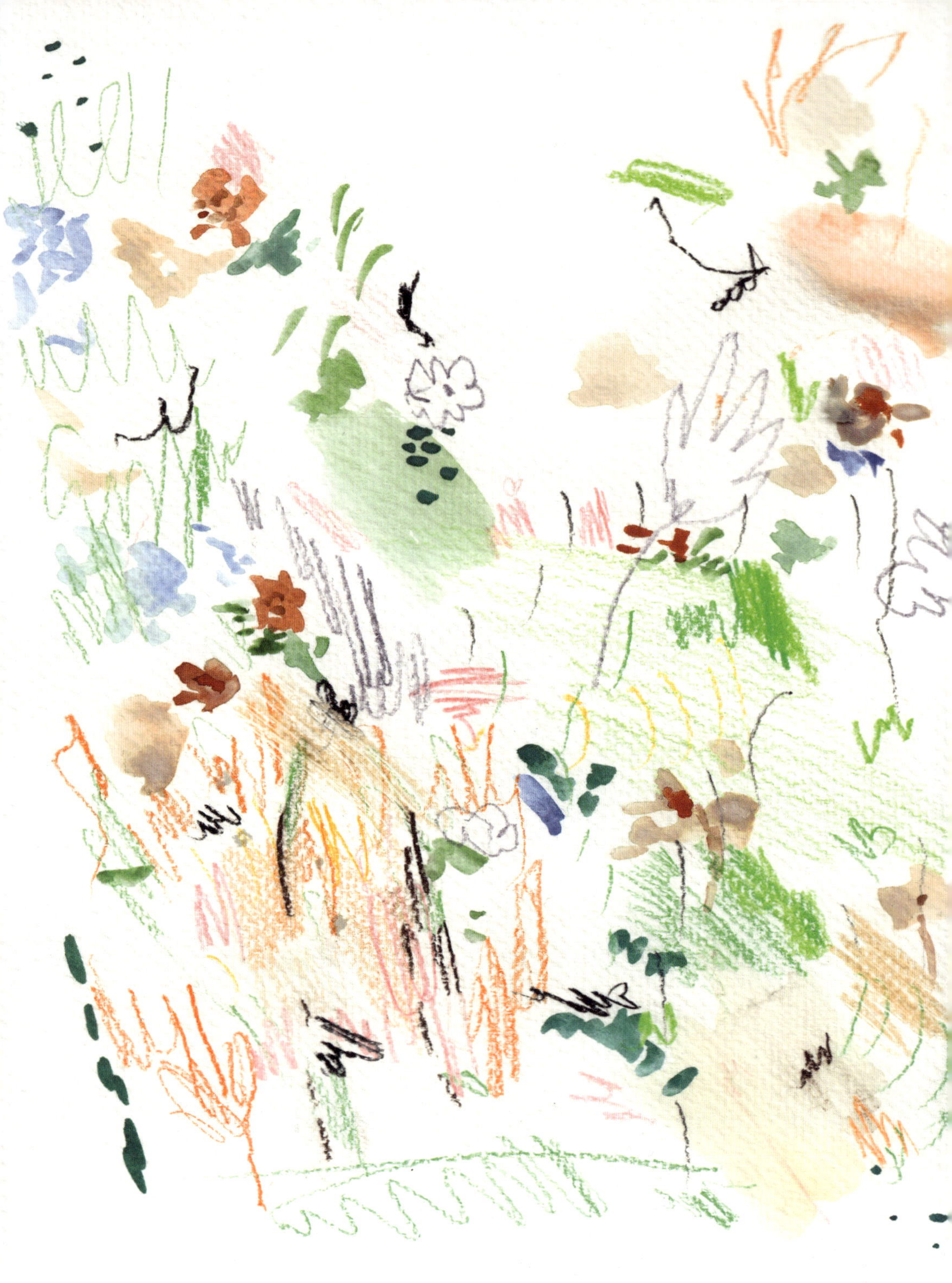

NATURE'S PERMISSION

Perfection is a heavy word,
and an even heavier burden.
I carried it for years.
On top of my shoulders. Inside my heart. Behind my eyes.

It weighed on me. Kept me small. Made me doubt.
Until one day I set it down,
just for a moment, to catch my breath.

Would you believe I felt lighter, taller, braver?
I saw that burden clearly,
Recognized it for what it was: an illusion.

I walked away
Imperfect.
Perfectly so.

Perhaps this is what grace means—
wildflowers never apologize for their colors,
the moon doesn't grieve its phases.
Your imperfections might be
the very doorway through which light enters.

IMPERFECT

IM PERFECT

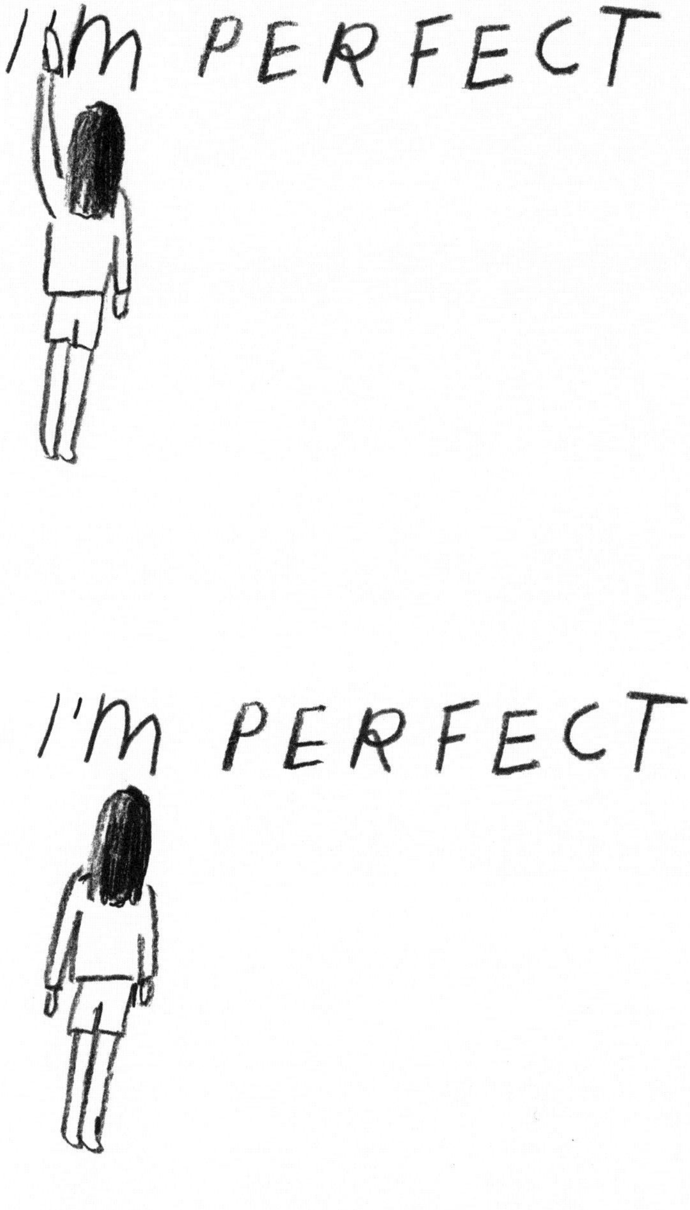

I'M PERFECT

I'M PERFECT

SOMETIMES I FEEL NOTHING.

SOMETIMES I FEEL EVERYTHING.

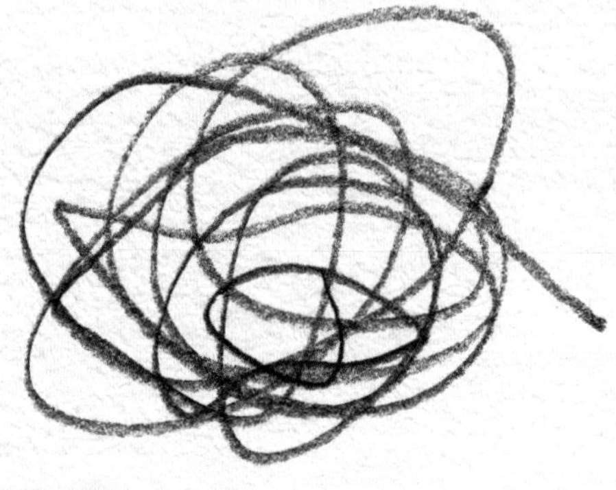

MIND FULL

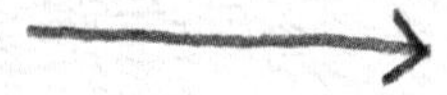

MINDFUL

TODAY I FOCUS

ON WHAT I

CAN DO,

NOT ON WHAT

I CANNOT.

THAT'S ME
IN THE
CORNER

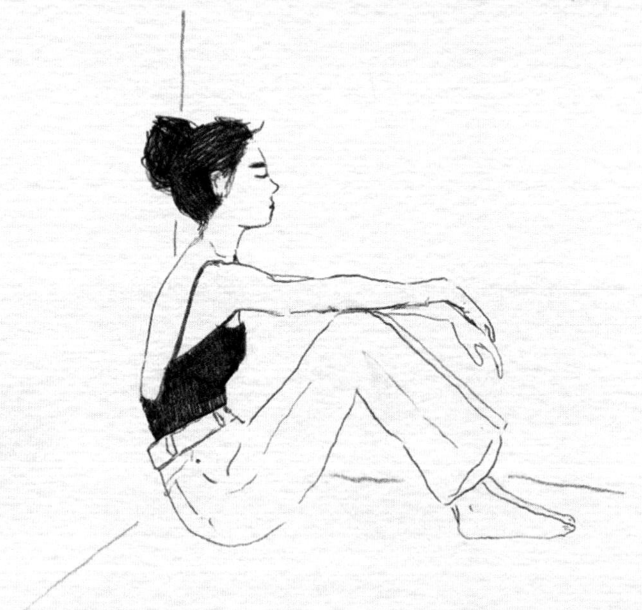

LOSING MY RELIGION

"Don't be afraid to be too much," he said as he watched me edit my words again. I was afraid of being too much. I was afraid that if I showed a hint of my true self, I might be rejected, judged, or, worst of all, found wanting. Better to stay composed; composure will keep me safe, acceptable, lovable.

This was my specialty, you see. Well-behaved straight out of the womb, all "pleases" and "no thank you's." I was a swan gliding across the pond, but underwater my feet were frantically paddling. I lay beside him while he slept, watching his breath come and go, my creature fear looming, that inner self we don't want to reveal.

We spend our entire lives mastering the different masks we put on. For decades I'd stayed hidden. He was the first to tell me not to shrink. So I held up that mirror, watched my layers of propriety fall away. No more strained smiles or swallowed words.

I was looking at the unpolished me, flawed, vulnerable, and beautifully human. I light a match to the ideas of "should" and "must." Flames lick at the edges of that carefully constructed world. And in the ashes of my old beliefs, I am found...

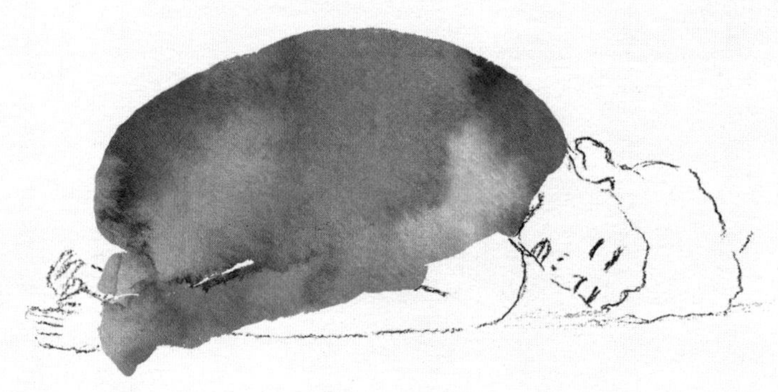

THERE WILL BE MOMENTS
OF SHRINKING...

THAT IN TURN
LEAD TO EXPANSION.

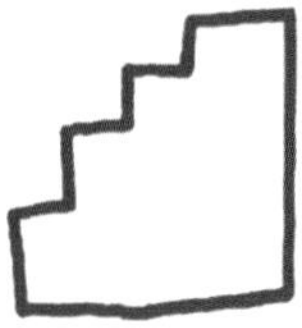

A STUMBLE
IS STILL
A STEP.

FALL DOWN
SEVEN TIMES,
GET UP
EIGHT.

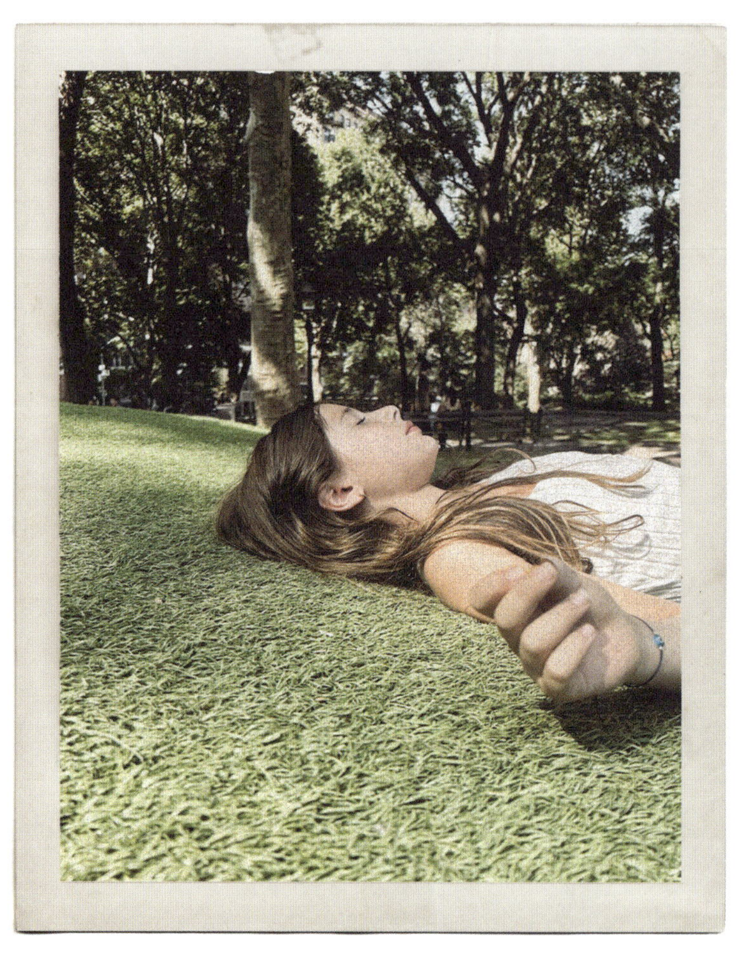

"I didn't want any flowers,
I only wanted to lie with my hands
turned up and be utterly empty.
How free it is, you have no idea
how free."

—Sylvia Plath

IN THE QUIET OF THE MORNING
BEFORE THE WORLD DEMANDS ANSWERS,
I SIT WITH MY HANDS OPEN,
PALMS HOLDING NOTHING BUT QUESTIONS.

THIS IS WHERE WE MEET HESITATION & HOPE,
EACH BREATH A SMALL REBELLION AGAINST
THE VOICE THAT SAYS "CANNOT."

I NOTICE HOW FEAR FEELS LIKE WISDOM
WHEN IT TELLS ME TO BE CAREFUL.
HOW "NOT READY" IS A PHRASE I KNOW WELL.

BUT WHAT IF - (HERE IS THE TEACHING)
THE TREMBLING ITSELF IS THE GATEWAY?
WHAT IF THE PAUSE, THIS SACRED UNCERTAINTY,
IS NOT THE OBSTACLE BUT THE PATH?

I PLACE MY HAND AGAINST MY HEART'S WILD KNOWING
FEEL HOW IT BEATS ANYWAY, DESPITE
ALL MY CAREFUL REASONS.

HERE, BETWEEN THINKING AND BEING,
LIES EVERYTHING I WAS AFRAID TO WANT.

TIME TO LET THE MORNING IN. TIME TO
LET THE MORNING BE.

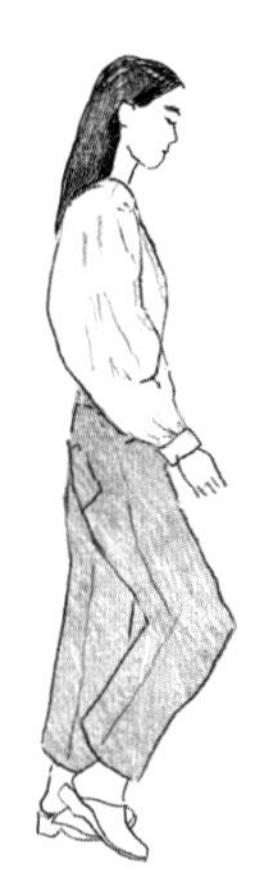

BEYOND THE DOUBT

Limitations are rarely about capability and almost always about narrative. The stories we tell ourselves—"I'm not the kind of person who could . . ." or "Someone like me doesn't . . ."—become prophecies that fulfill themselves.

What I've learned is that "I think I can't" is never the end of the story—it's merely a chapter. Each time I've pushed beyond a perceived limitation, I've discovered not just new capability, but a different version of myself emerging.

The dissolution of these boundaries isn't a one-time breakthrough, but a continuous practice. The work unfolds gradually—prying fingers loose from the safety rail, taking one step beyond the familiar. With each small venture past perceived limits, the territory of possibility expands. The "I think I can't" softens into "perhaps I might," and eventually, wonderfully, into "I already am."

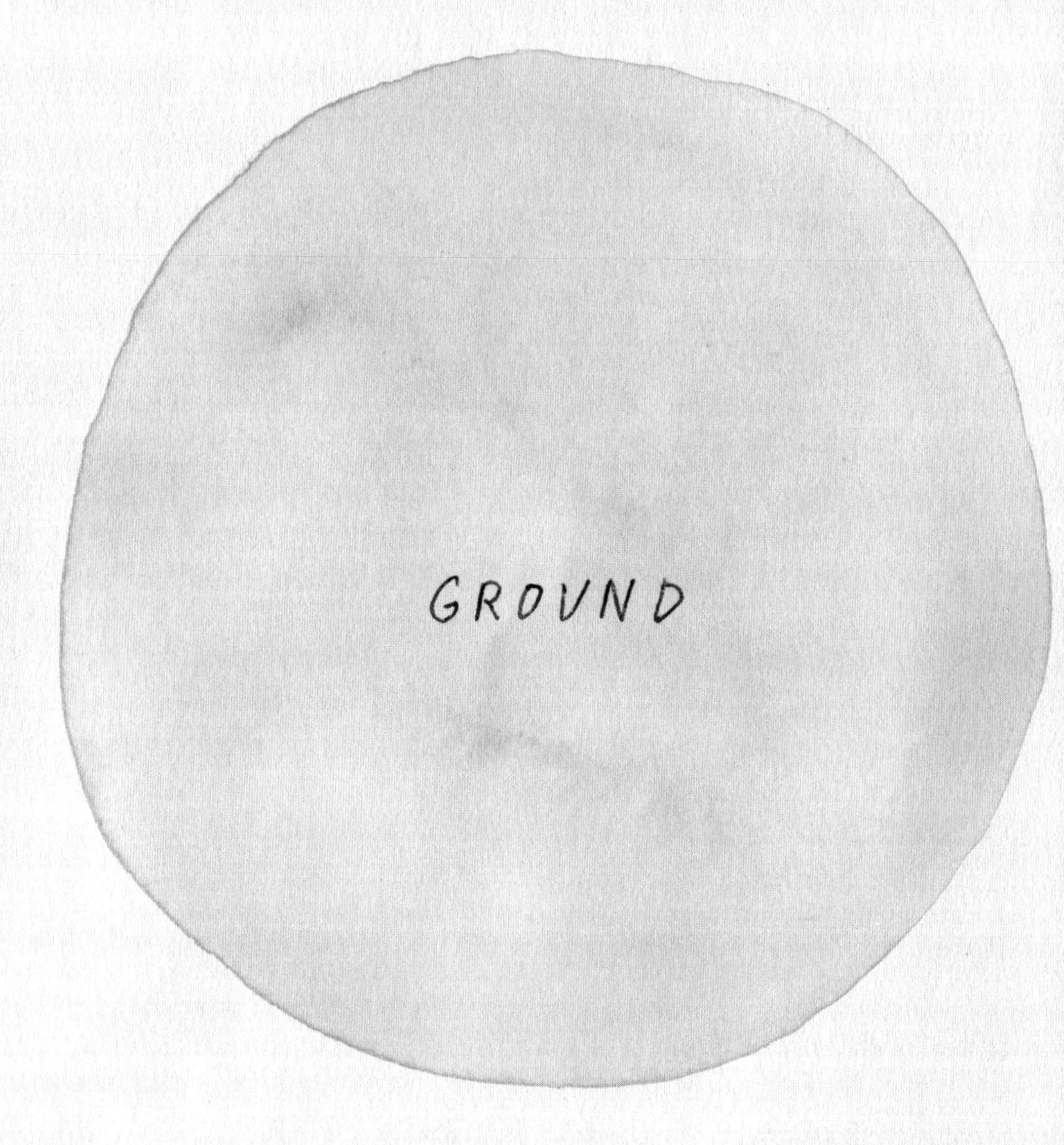
GROUND

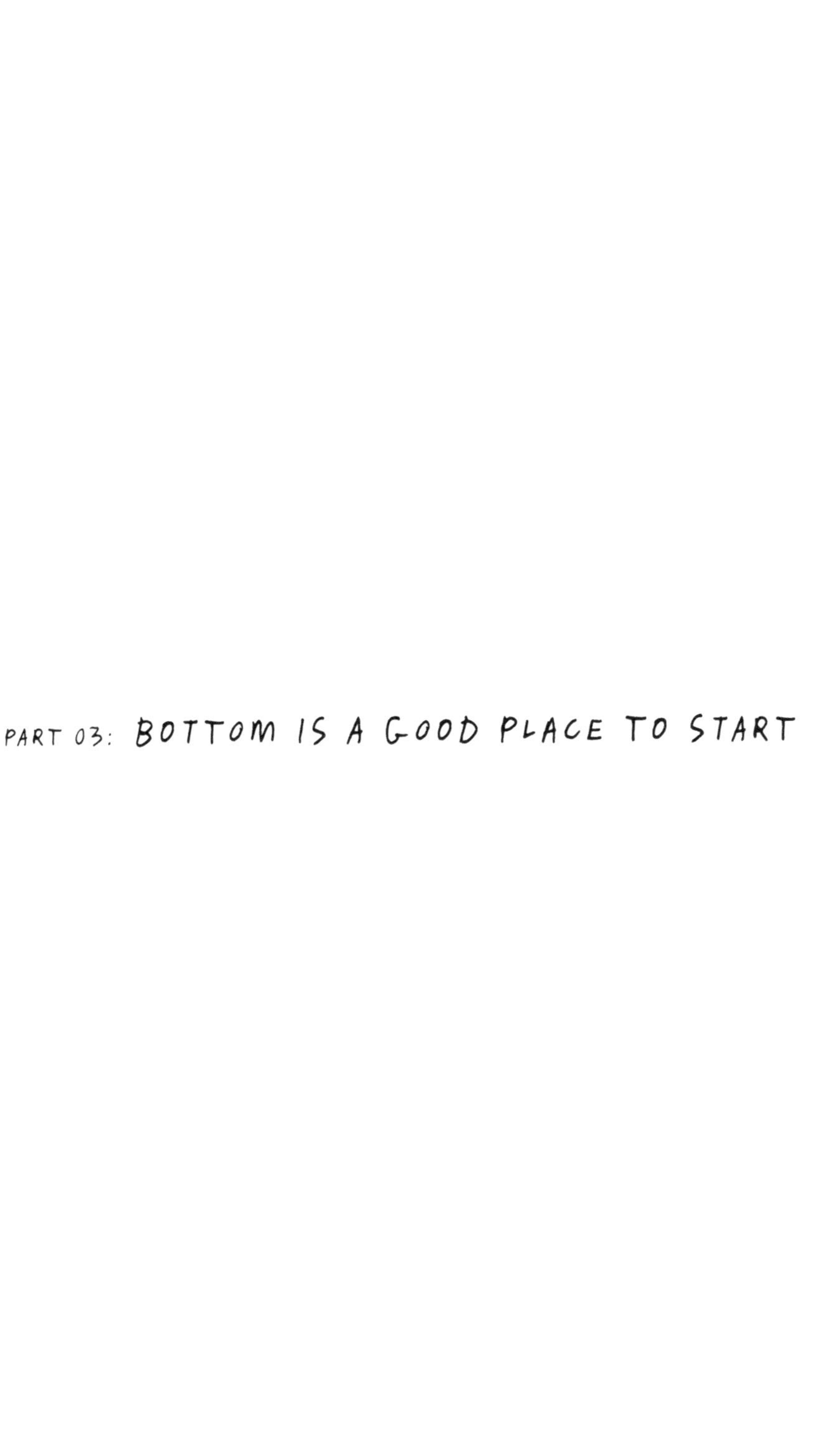
PART 03: BOTTOM IS A GOOD PLACE TO START

GROUND

I often encounter moments that strip me bare, leaving me feeling desolate and lost. I have come to refer to these times as "my bottoms"—when plans crumble, certainties dissolve, and I find myself drowning in the sea of unfamiliar and uncomfortable territory.

Yet, paradoxically, it is often in these moments of greatest despair that I discover the seeds of profound transformation and renewal. For when we lose everything we thought defined us, we are forced to confront our essential selves. The facade of success, the armor of our carefully constructed identities, and the comfort of our routines all fall away. We're left with nothing but our raw, vulnerable humanity. This state, though painful, is also the fertile ground for rebirth.

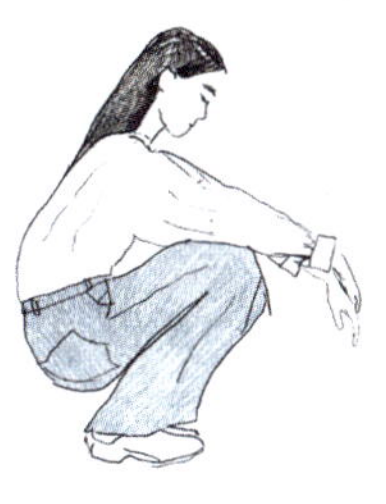

YOUR BAD DAYS
ARE PART OF
YOUR GOOD LIFE.

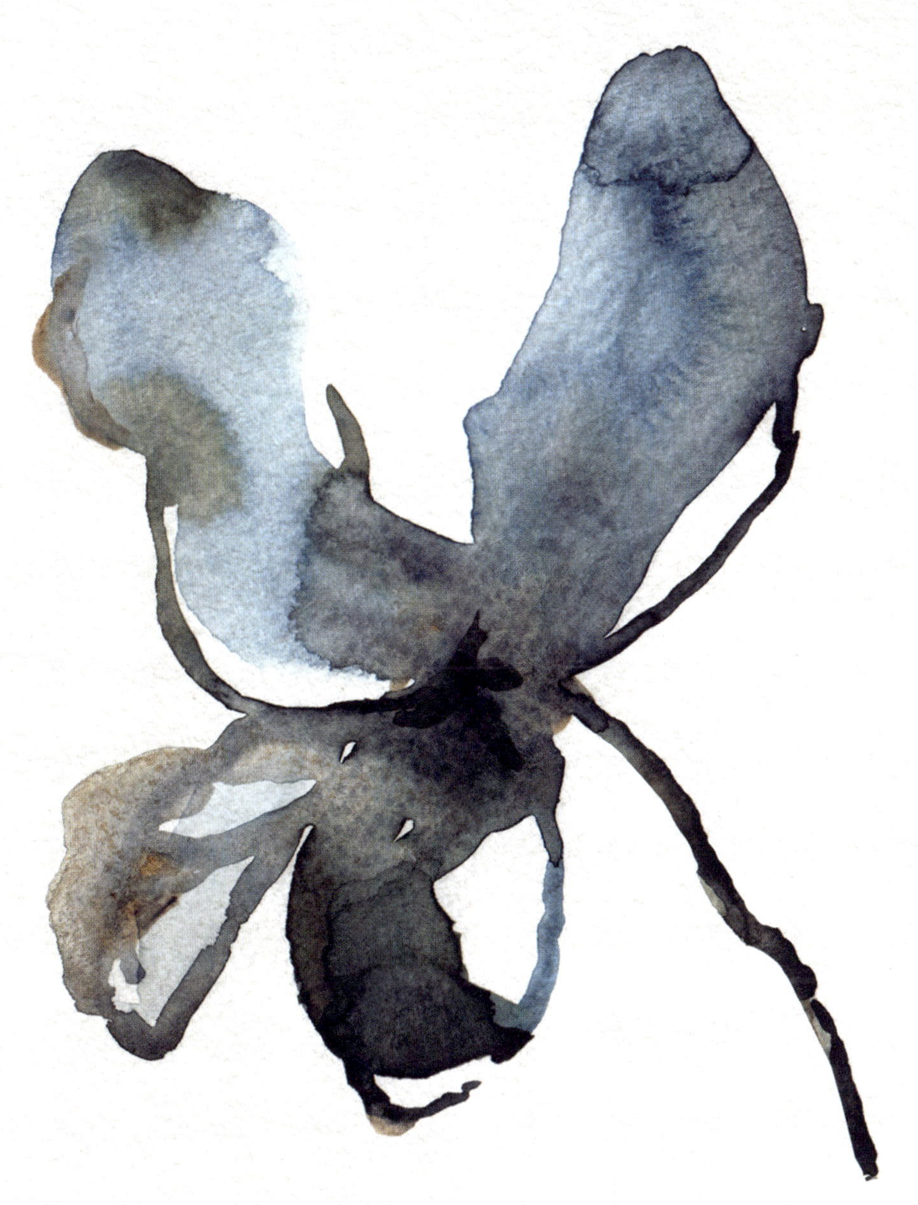

THE FLOWER YOU SEE TODAY
STARTED AS A
TINY SEED WHO
BELIEVED IN TOMORROW.

Truth knows where to settle—
always down, always deep.
I've stopped fearing these depths.
Now I fear only being too light
to earn my way to bottom.
Some weights are worth carrying.
Some depths are worth reaching.

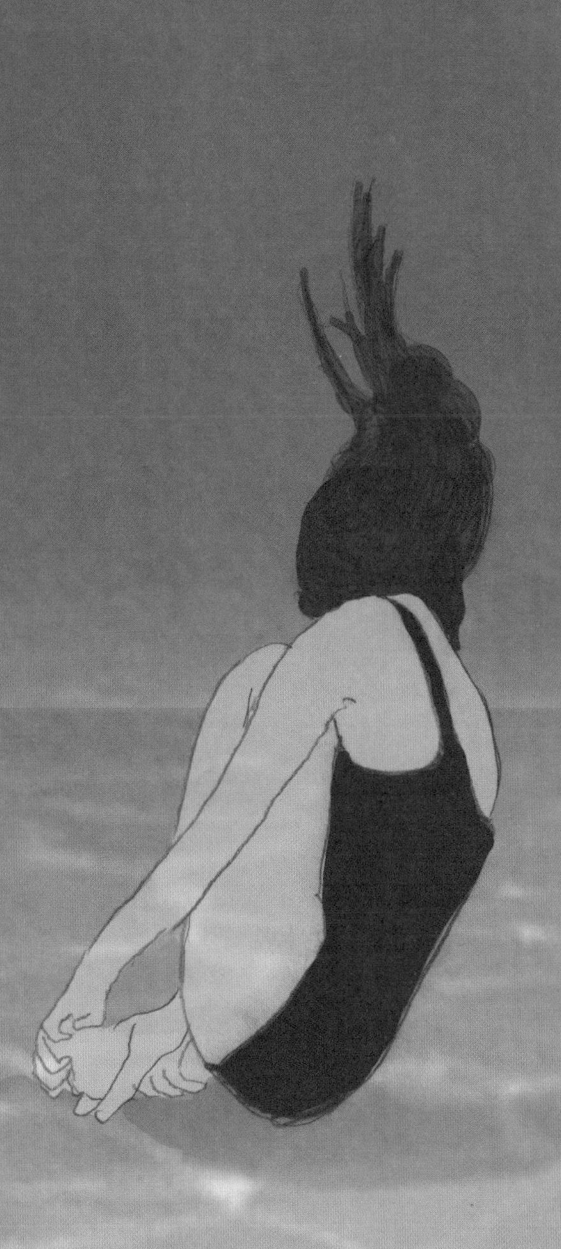

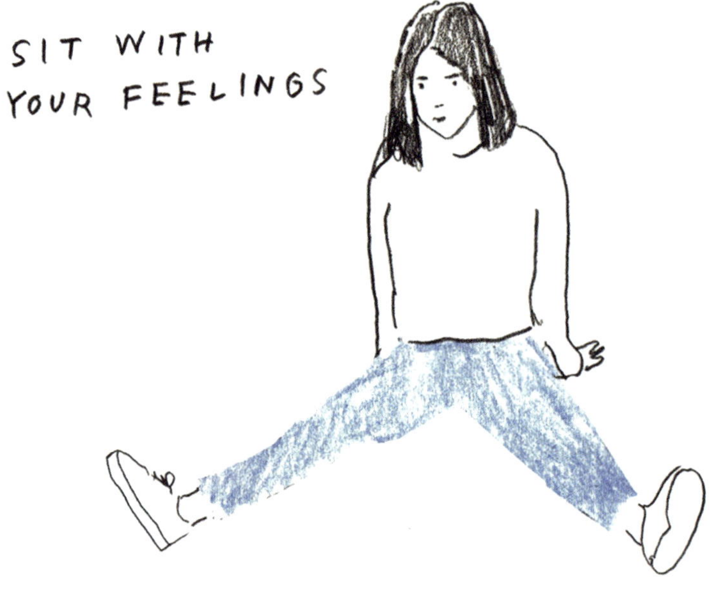
SIT WITH
YOUR FEELINGS

The fear of an unfulfilled life often stems from our tendency to suppress emotions, especially uncomfortable ones. But our emotions are messengers carrying maps to places we need to go.

Listen to your anger—it knows when someone has crossed a line worth defending. Notice your frustration—it's showing you where to dig deeper, where to try another way. Even boredom has something to say—it whispers that you've outgrown this moment and need to stretch toward something new.

What if, instead of running, we turned to face these feelings? What if we asked them: Why are you here? What are you trying to show me?

When we numb ourselves—with scrolling, with noise, with being busy—we lose our way. We silence the voices meant to guide us, the emotional awareness that serves as our compass, pointing us toward what matters.

Our wholeness lives in feeling everything. The uncomfortable truth is that our pain and our purpose are often twin travelers on the same road.

Sit with your feelings. They know the way.

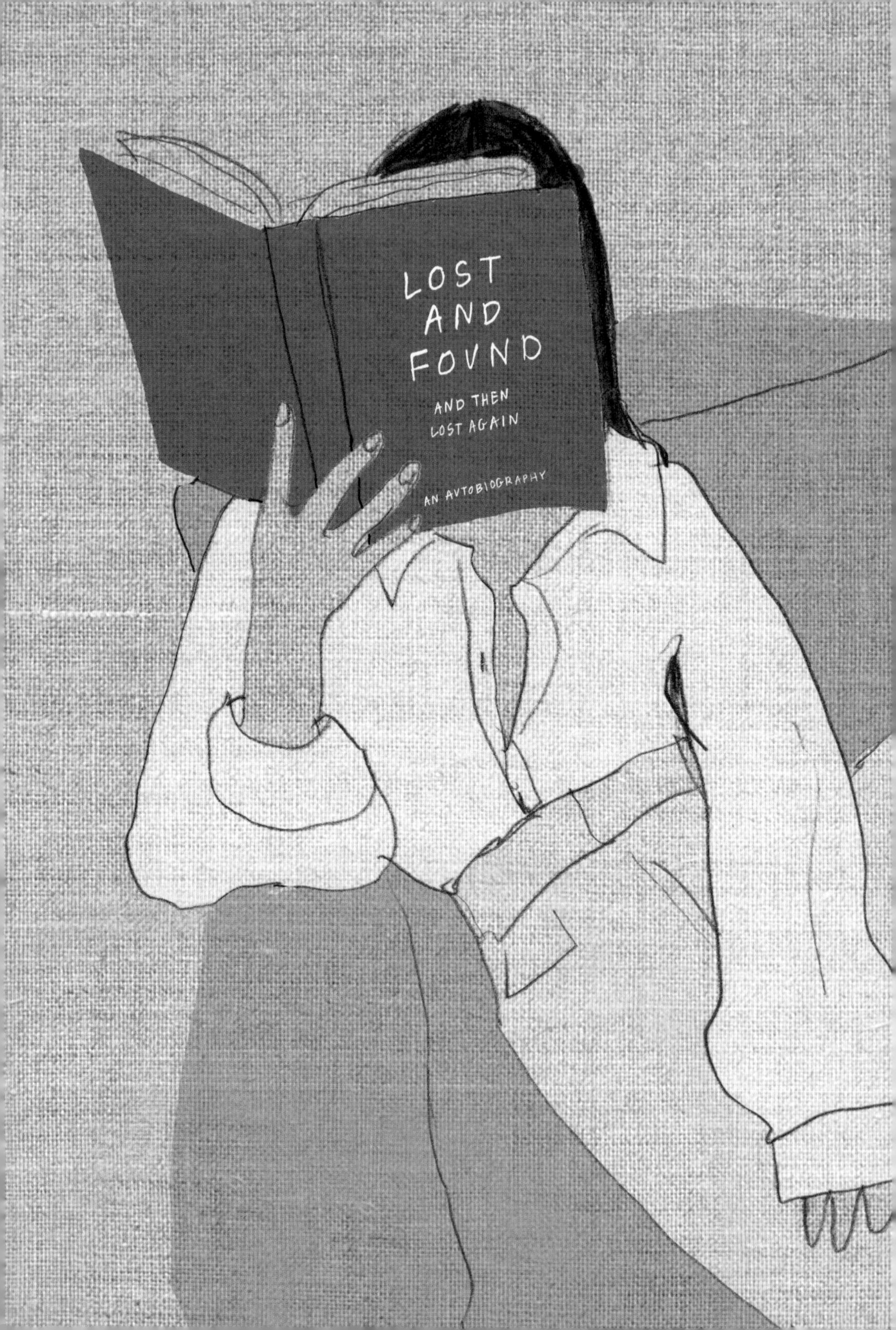
LOST
AND
FOUND
AND THEN
LOST AGAIN
AN AUTOBIOGRAPHY

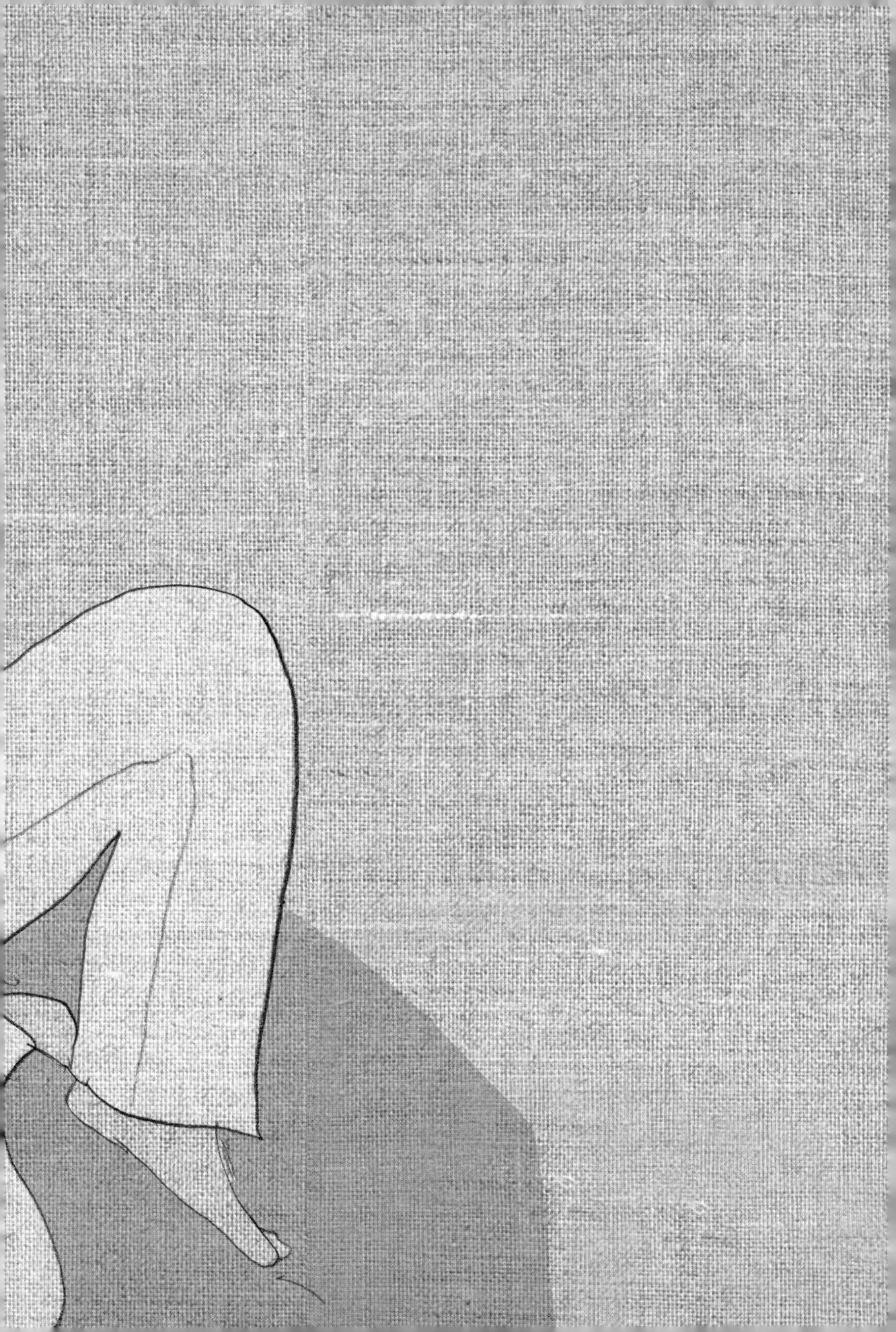

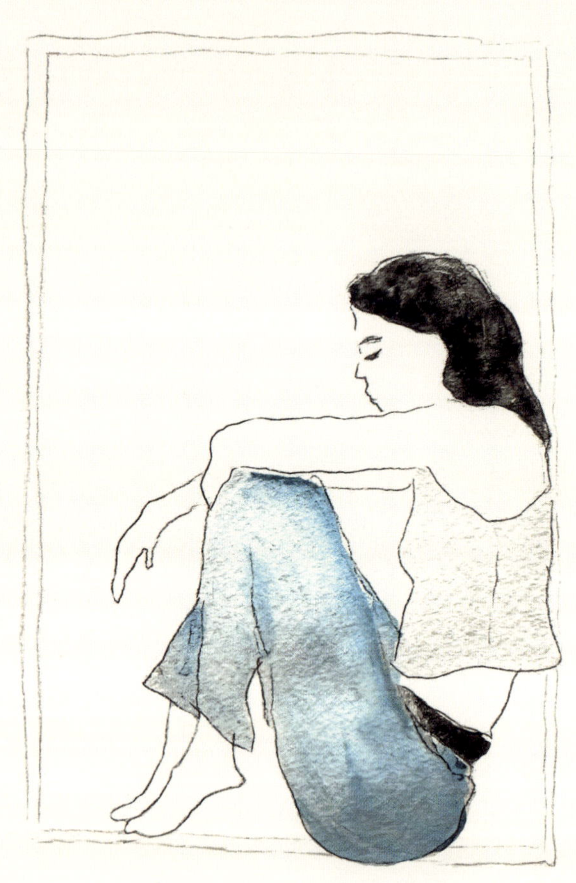

PAUSE.

I'M STILL HERE

"Eventually, everything connects."
This is something I scribbled a few years ago,
and I still believe it to be true.
But with time and understanding,
I have learned that there is a small caveat:
You have to be open to letting everything connect.

So take a moment to breathe,
to know yourself,
to remember that you, too,
are part of everything.

PASEO ENCANTADO / SANTE FE

STAY

There was a crack across his windshield.
I noticed it when I climbed into his dusty truck.
It spanned from the driver's side all the way over
to the edge of my right shoulder.
He said there was no reason to fix it;
it would just happen again.
"Rocks always kick up from the road."

I hadn't been back to this place since 2019,
thirty-two days after my mother left this beautiful
and, also, painful world.
As we drove up into the ruddy terrain,
I was overwhelmed by how much memory the vastness held.
My heart swelled like a balloon.
One that was being filled up with hurt,
but also some forgiveness.

We walked along a narrow path.
My eyes recognized the shapes and colors from before.
In between then and now,
I'd been trying to patch up my own cracks,
paint them in so they couldn't be seen.

But as I looked out on the mountains,
on that expanse that now wrapped its arms around me,
cradled me the way I wanted her to
and pulled me closer into its beauty,
I understood that I had to let the rocks keep kicking up.
I understood that some cracks need to stay.

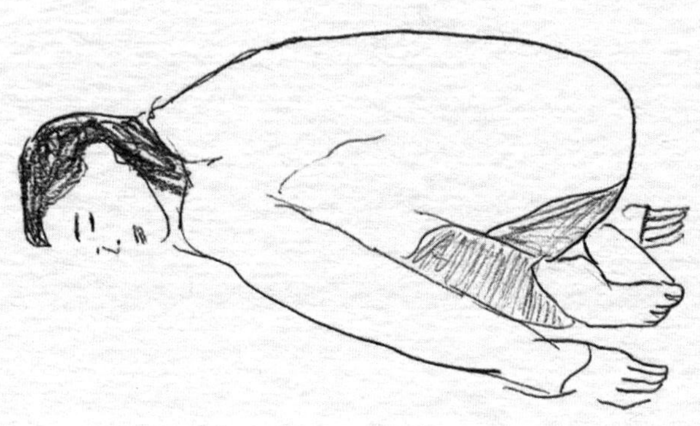

TAKING THINGS
SLOW TODAY.

JUST BECAUSE
I'M STILL FIGURING
IT OUT DOES NOT
MEAN I'M WASTING
TIME.

OUR JOURNEY IS NOT FIXED

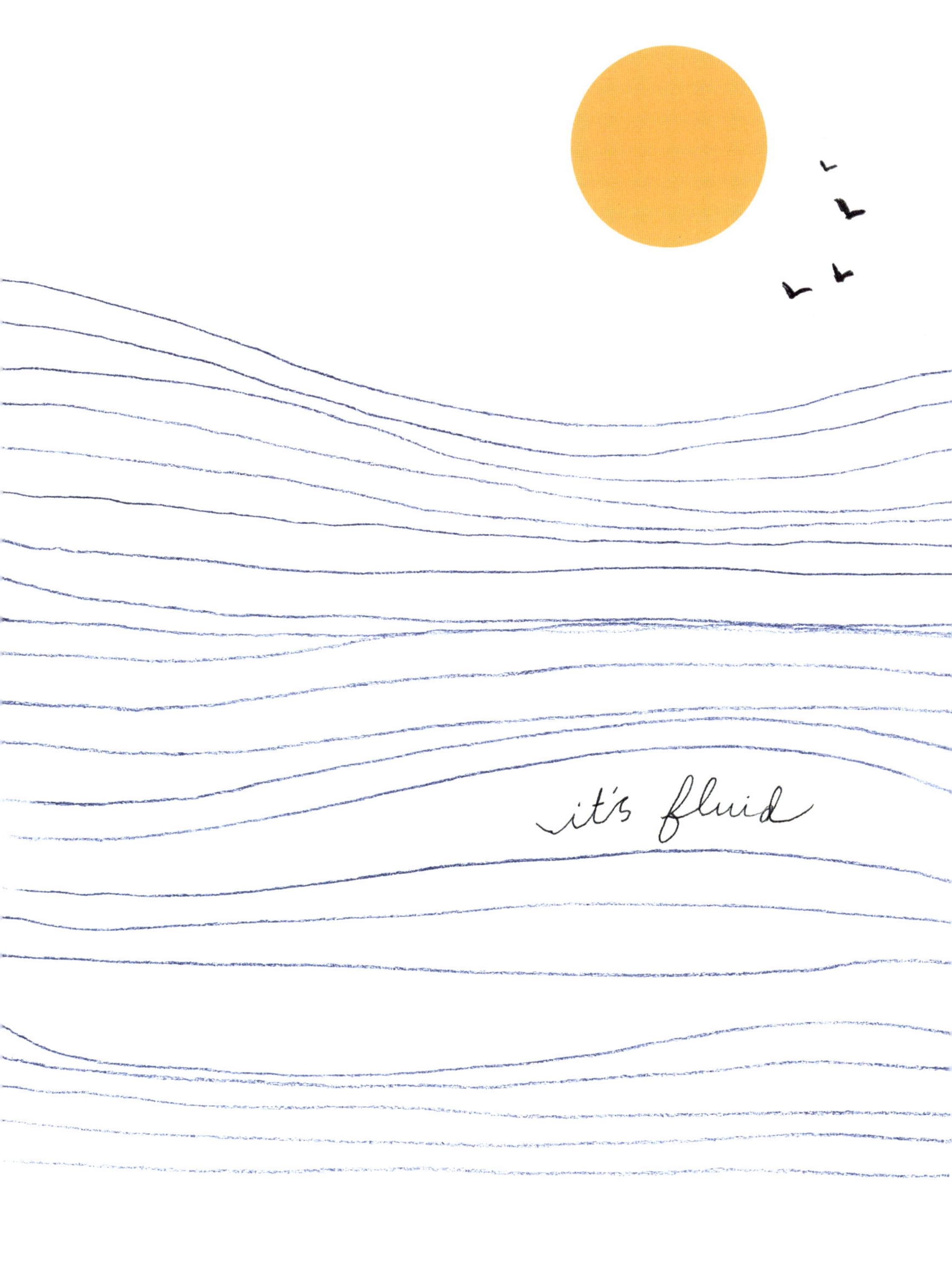
it's fluid

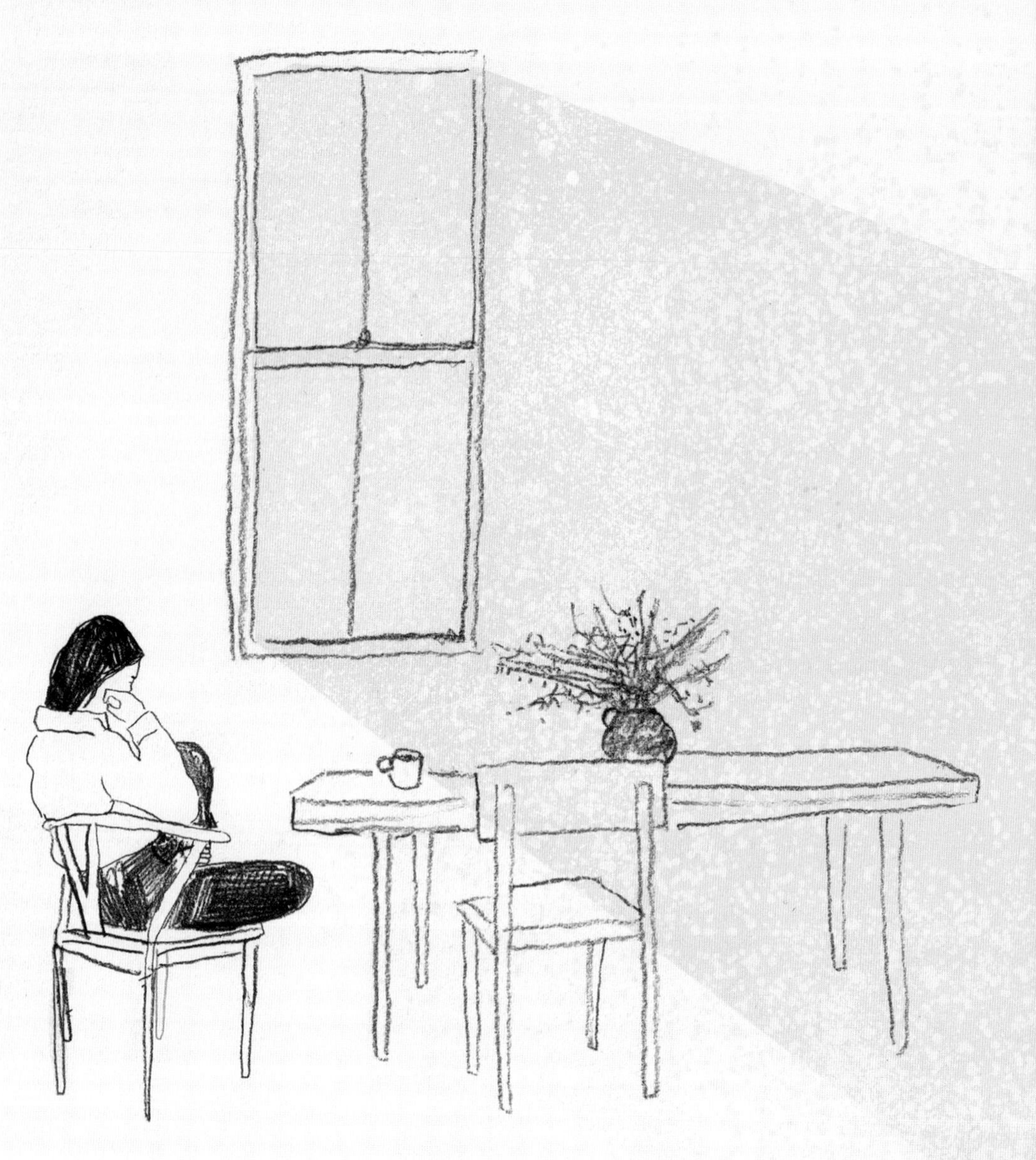

THE GIFT OF EMPTY HOURS

Morning light spills across the empty table,
and hours stretch before you, like blank pages.
I've been here too, watching shadows lengthen
across a quiet room.

What will you do with this ordinary Saturday?
Every moment doesn't need filling with noise.
Every chair doesn't need someone to warm it.

What else can you do but sit with this ache,
this honest solitude, until it teaches you what
loneliness has always known—
that even in emptiness, something grows.

And so we go on, planting new rituals
in the soil of old memories,
watching different flowers
bloom in familiar light.

seeds of

TRANSFORMATION

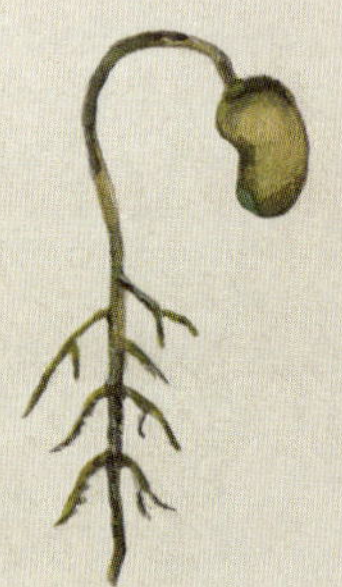

PATIENCE REQUIRED /
DARKNESS ESSENTIAL

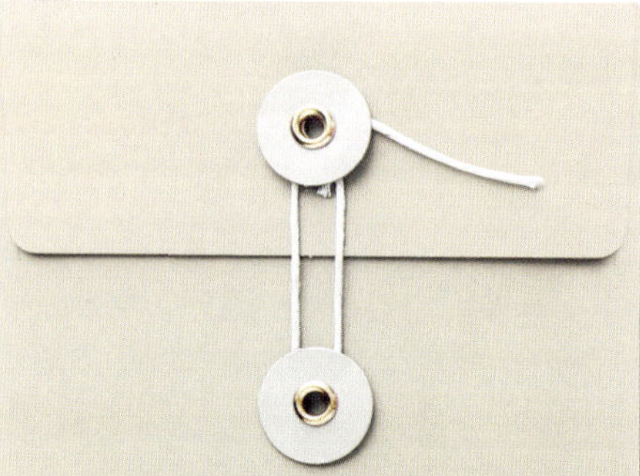

PLANTING INSTRUCTIONS:

Bury deeply. Allow pressure & darkness.
Wait without expectation.
Trust what you cannot see.

HARVESTING:

Growth occurs invisibly
long before evidence appears.

In the dark beneath the weight
are where seeds begin their journey.

MAY THE GOOD THINGS
IN LIFE FIND YOU,
AND WHEN THEY DO
MAY YOU HAVE THE
ABILITY TO RECOGNIZE
THAT YOU ARE DESERVING
OF EVERY ONE OF THEM.

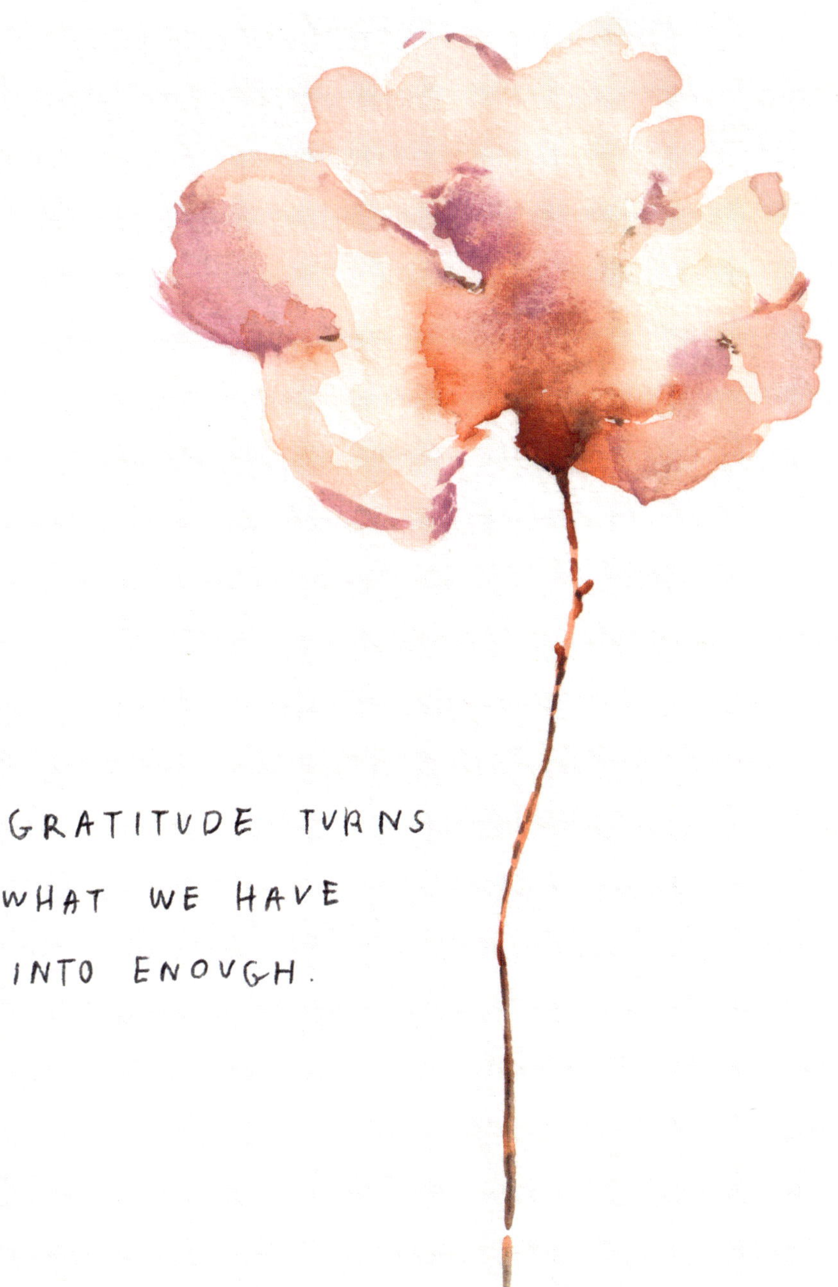
GRATITUDE TURNS
WHAT WE HAVE
INTO ENOUGH.

PERMISSION SLIP

AUTHENTIC BEING

Last Name First Name

Date NOW Room TO GROW

Purpose

TO HONOR WHAT FEELS RIGHT TO ME

PERMISSION SLIP

AUTHENTIC BEING

Last Name First Name

Date NOW Room TO GROW

Purpose TO RELEASE EXPECTATIONS AND EMBRACE MYSELF FULLY.

You have permission to: breathe deeply, forgive yourself, trust your journey, embrace uncertainty and bloom in your own time.

You have permission to be here,
to rest, to not know,
to let go of who you were,
to wait for what's next.

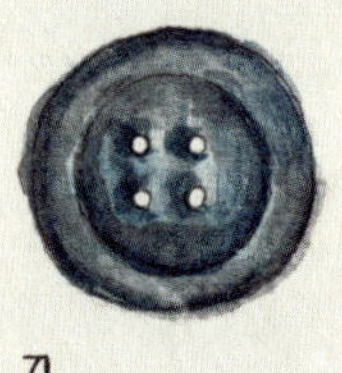

A BUTTON THAT HELD
COCO'S COAT CLOSED

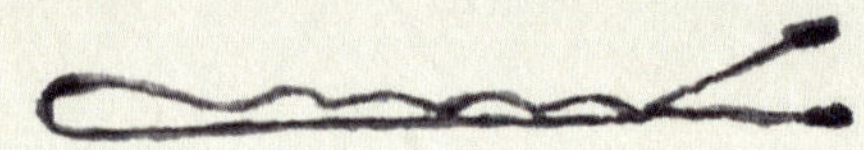

A BOBBY PIN FROM
MY MOTHER'S HAIR

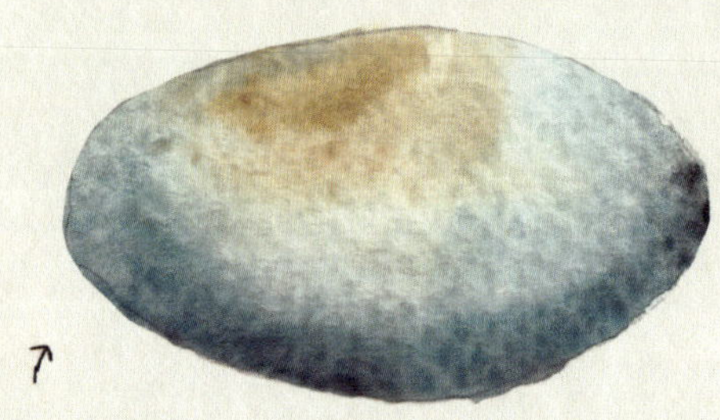

A SMOOTH RIVER STONE
TOUCHED BY COUNTLESS WATERS

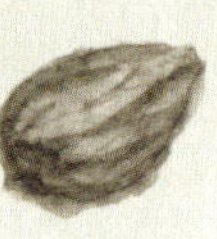

A SEED REMINDING ME
OF POTENTIAL EVEN IN
DORMANT TIMES

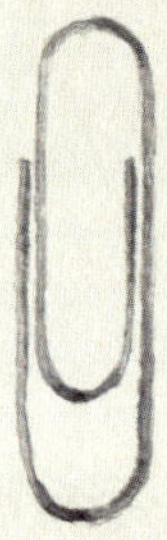

A PAPER CLIP FROM NOTES
FOR MY FIRST BOOK

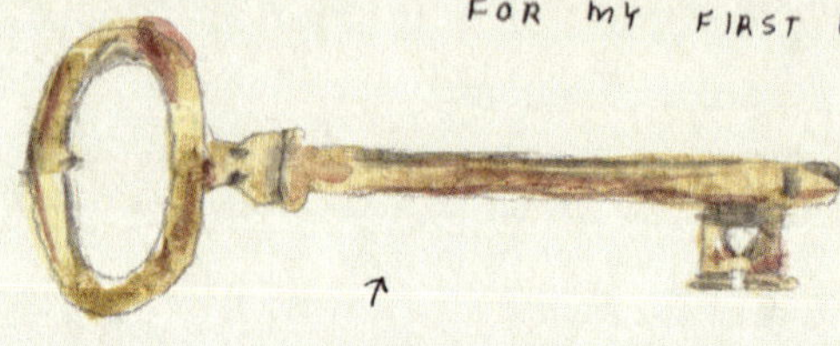

A SINGLE FEATHER FOUND
ON A DIFFICULT DAY

A SMALL KEY
TO A FORGOTTEN LOCK

When we find ourselves at the bottom, ordinary treasures reveal their extraordinary nature. A button carries the memory of comfort. A seed holds possibility without guarantee. A stone reminds us that smoothness comes from weathering.

These small things, once invisible in our hurried lives, become companions when we have nowhere else to look but here, nowhere to be but now.

BEYOND THE GROUND

What feels like failure often contains the possibility of something else entirely. When everything external gets swept away—the job, the relationship, the carefully curated version of yourself—what's left is startlingly simple: just you, still breathing, still here. I've learned that these moments serve as both ending and beginning. One version of yourself dies so another can emerge. The discomfort isn't the problem—it's the ground for transformation. The breaking down doesn't just clear space for rebuilding; it provides the raw elements—the humility, the clarity—that become the foundation of whatever comes next. In losing who I thought I was, I discover materials I never knew I possessed.

This emptying and refilling follows its own rhythm. I've gotten better at sitting in the apparent void, trusting that it contains possibilities I can't see yet.

Starting from the bottom brings a particular kind of clarity. With fewer distractions, you can finally hear the voice that's always been there, pointing toward what actually matters. The path forward rarely looks like what you planned, but it becomes clear that it's the one you're meant to walk.

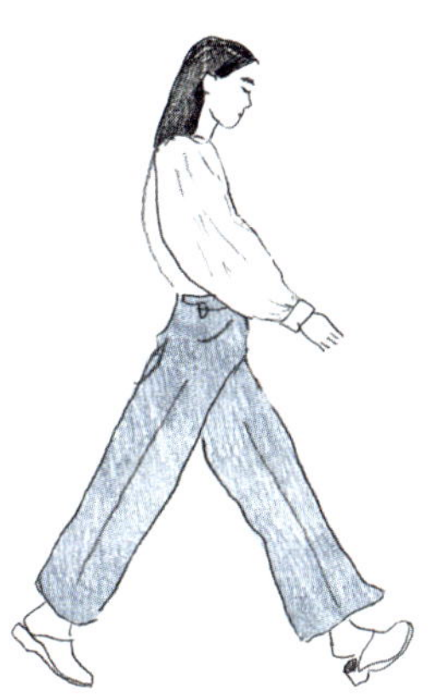

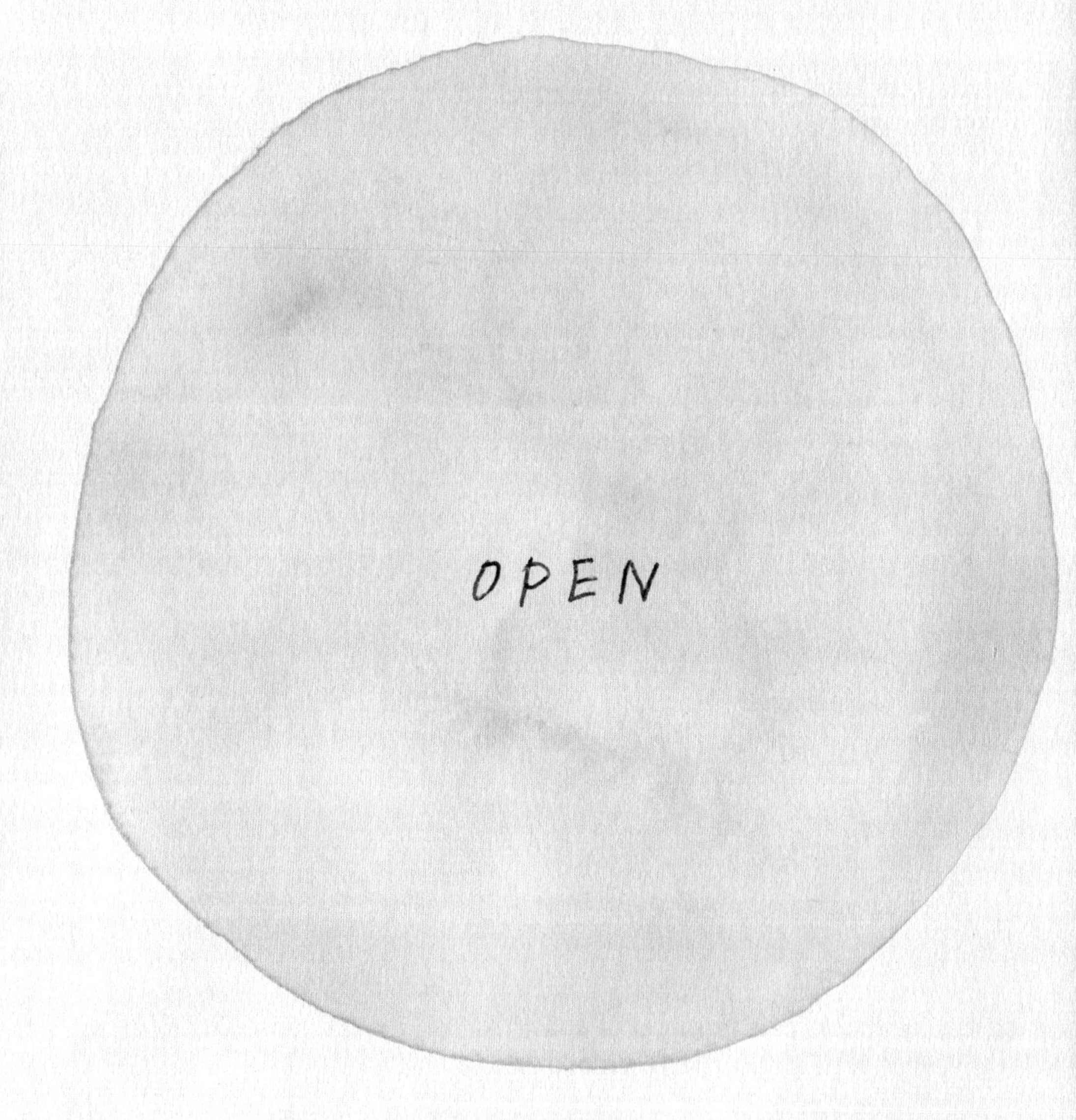
OPEN

PART 04: PRESENCE IS THE BEST PRESENT

OPEN

I get lost in my own life more often than I care to admit. Not geographically lost, but temporally—caught between yesterday's regrets and tomorrow's anxieties, missing today entirely. I keep looking for answers everywhere except where I am standing.

This disconnection didn't happen overnight. Somewhere along the way, I learned that the present moment was dangerous ground—too raw, too uncertain, too demanding of actual feeling. It became easier to live in the story of my life rather than the experience of it. What we're really avoiding when we flee the now isn't boredom or stillness—it's the uncomfortable truth of our actual feeling. The present moment asks us to meet life without the buffer of our narratives, and that can feel like standing naked in a storm.

But when I do manage to arrive—really arrive—in the present moment, something shifts. Quietly. Subtly. Like shadows shifting across a wall. The details I usually miss come into focus. I notice things. I pay attention. It's simple and surprisingly difficult.

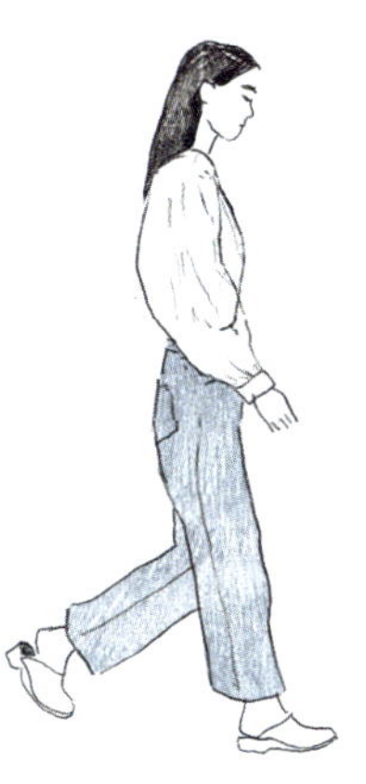

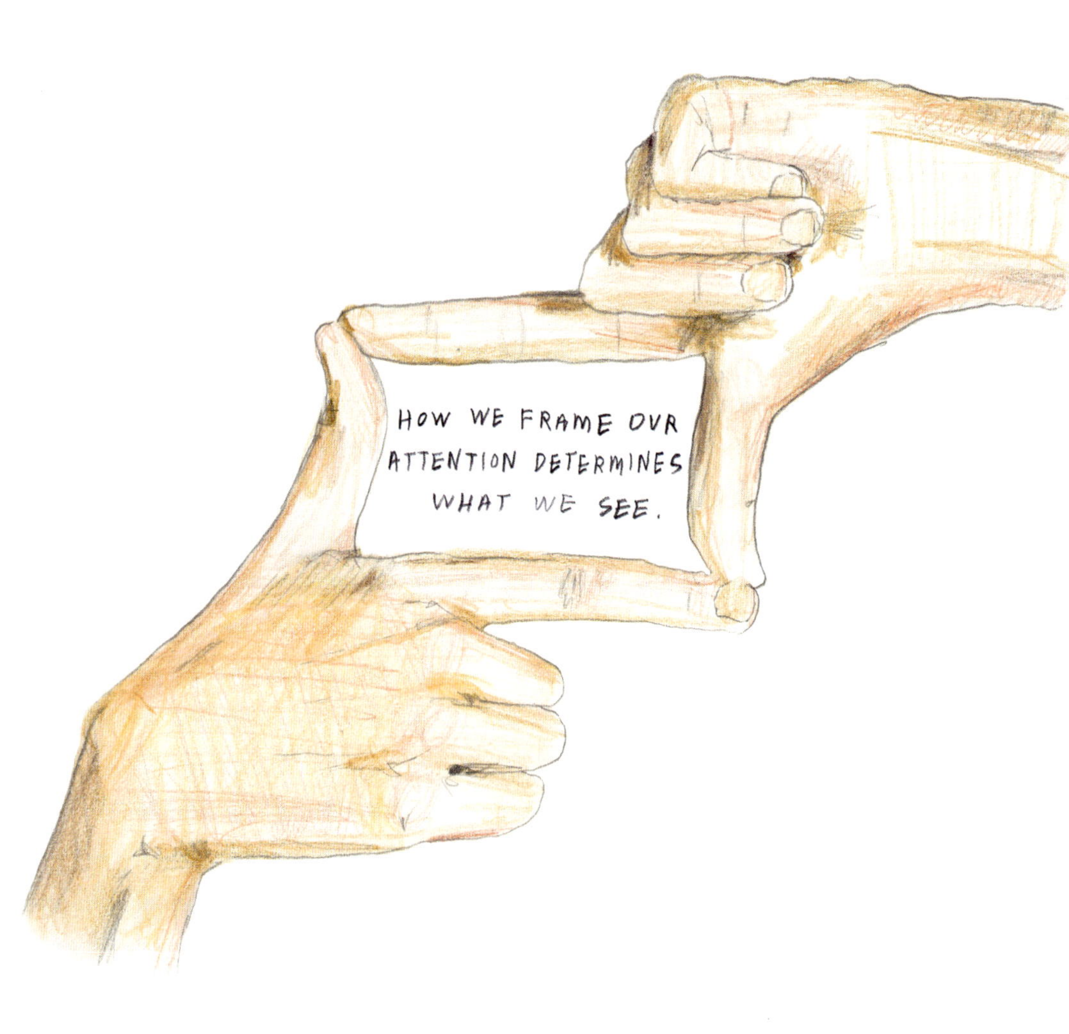
HOW WE FRAME OUR
ATTENTION DETERMINES
WHAT WE SEE.

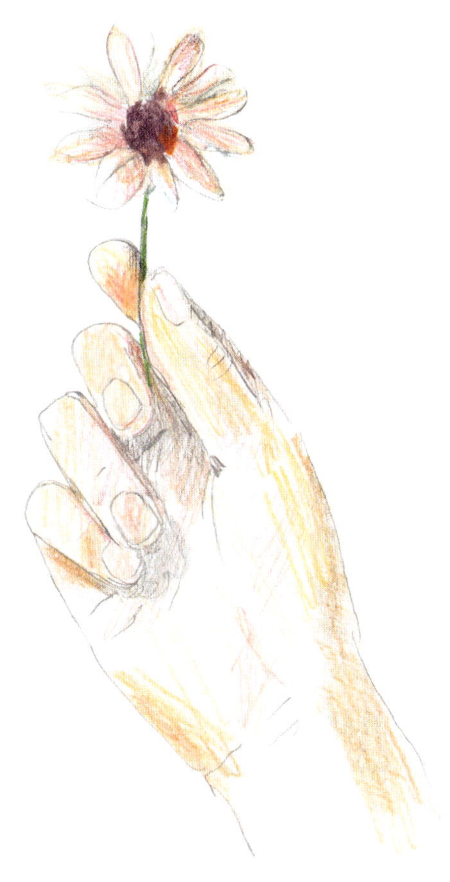

THE WORLD IS FULL OF BEAUTY
WAITING TO BE NOTICED.

LET GO OF
HOW IT LOOKS.

TELL ME,
HOW DOES
IT FEEL?

THE WORLD DOES NOT NEED ME TODAY.

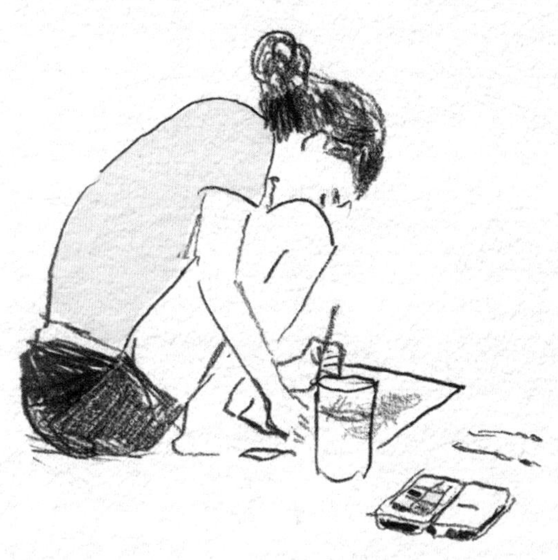

I don't need to be
anyone's lighthouse today.
The world spins perfectly well
without my watching.

The hours stretch out,
empty of purpose,
complete in their own
simple way.

This is all there is:
the soft hum of being,
asking nothing
of anyone.

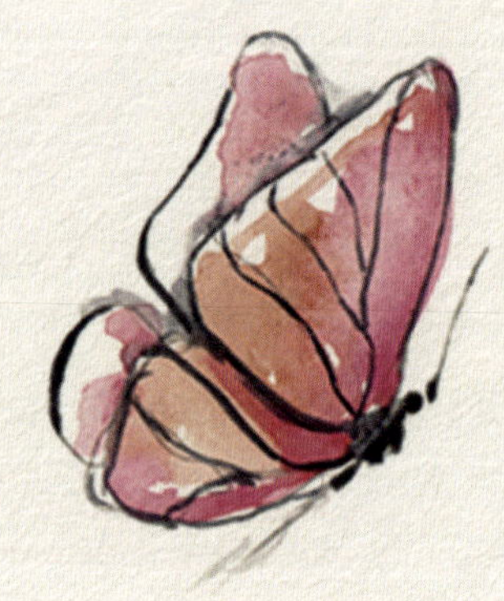

A butterfly appeared at my window and spent twenty minutes beating its wings against the closed glass. Over and over, it threw itself at the barrier, desperate to reach the garden on the other side, trapped by something it couldn't understand. Two feet away, another window stood wide open to the same garden.

I watched this small struggle and recognized something familiar. How often do I exhaust myself pushing against what won't budge, while missing what's already available?

Sometimes the way forward isn't through the obstacle. Sometimes it's around it, beside it, or along a path we haven't noticed yet.

The butterfly eventually found the open window. Not through force, but by pausing long enough to sense a different current of air—the freedom that had been there all along.

Maybe that's all any of us need—a moment to stop pushing and start noticing what else might be possible.

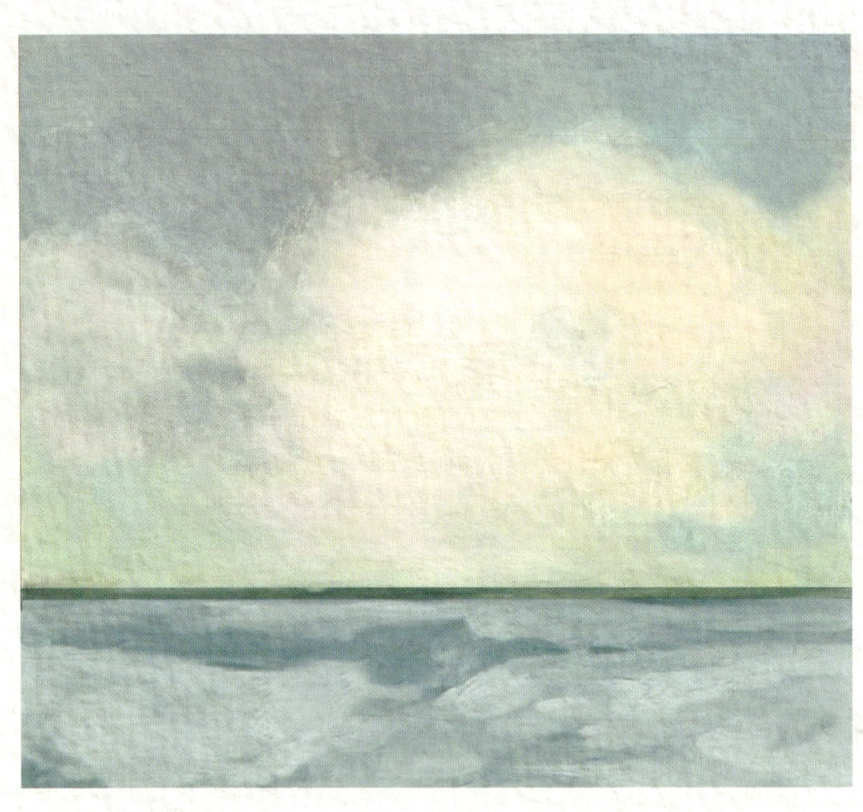

TAKE TIME TO LOOK.
SEE THE BEAUTY AROUND YOU.

AGE BRINGS A
CERTAIN MAGIC -

THE ABILITY TO SEE
THE EXTRAORDINARY
IN THE ORDINARY MOMENTS
WE ONCE RUSHED PAST.

So many voices in this world: the market sellers with their ripe promises, the billboards painting dreams across the sky, the endless parade of better lives we could be living.

My daughter's hand on my wrist is warm as fresh bread. The world spins its constant wheel of desire, while here, in this small moment, everything I need breathes quietly beside me.

Remember you must die, the ancient ones whisper through leaves and wind and passing seasons. Remember you must live, my daughter's fingers say, tiny prophets pressing against my restless skin.

Everything I ever wanted was always this simple: the weight of a hand, the courage to stay in one moment long enough to taste its truth, the wisdom to know when enough has bloomed into plenty.

EVERYTHING
I EVER
WANTED.

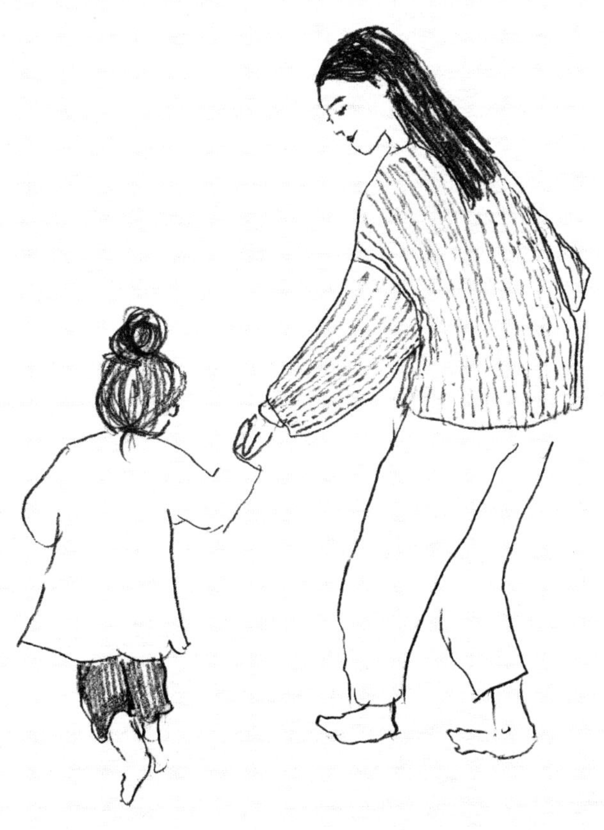

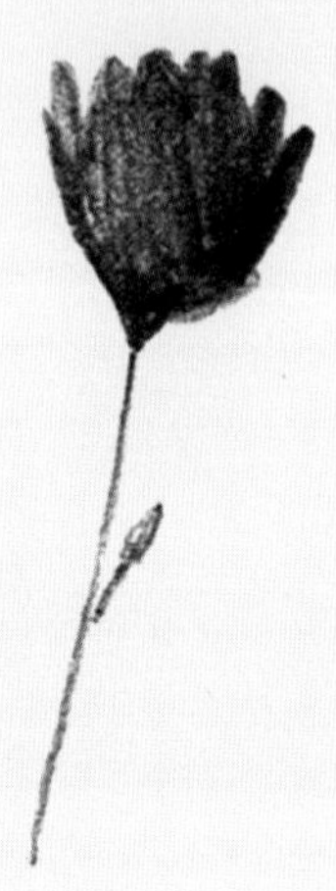

"IF WE COULD SEE THE MIRACLE OF A SINGLE FLOWER CLEARLY, OUR WHOLE WORLD WOULD CHANGE."

– JACK KORNFIELD

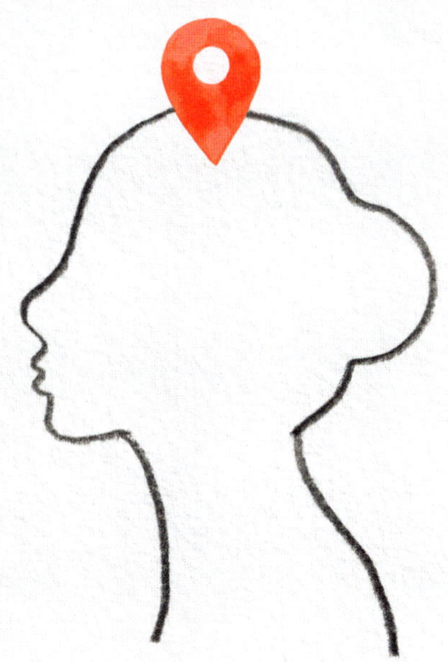

THE MOST IMPORTANT
REAL ESTATE YOU'LL OWN
IS YOUR MIND.

TOO LATE
TO BE
IN A
HURRY

Something shifts in midlife. I find myself caught between still feeling like I should be rushing toward something and understanding that time has weight now. It's easy to think it's too late for the things I haven't done yet.

But frantic rushing rarely gets me where I want to go. Maybe this is when I can slow down enough to notice what I've built, what I've learned, and what actually matters.

When I stop fighting where I am—all the messy, complicated parts—something opens up. I start living my actual life instead of some future version of it.

NOWHERE TO GO.

NOTHING TO BE.

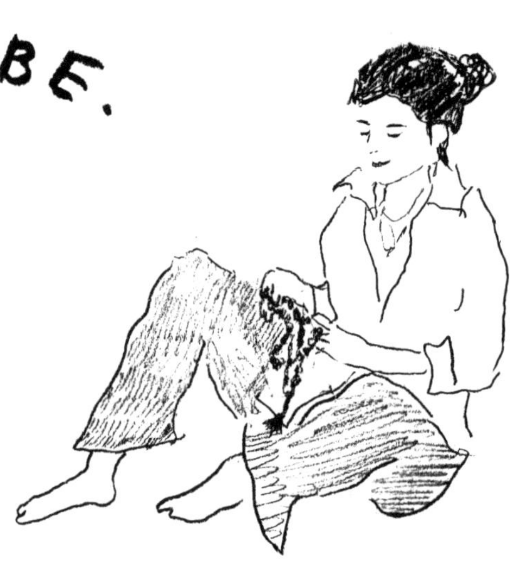

"Nowhere to go. Nothing to be." I whispered these words to Coco on unsettled nights, when sleep felt too far away. When her mind was still full of the day's stories and tomorrow's possibilities.

The words would float in the darkness of her room, simple and true. A reminder that this moment was enough—that the world could wait, that being here was all that mattered. I watched as they settled over her like a familiar blanket, how they helped her find her way to sleep.

Now, on nights when my own mind won't quiet, I find myself whispering these same words. "Nowhere to go. Nothing to be." Words I learned by teaching them to her.

Funny how that works—how the gentleness we show others teaches us to be gentle with our own restless hearts.

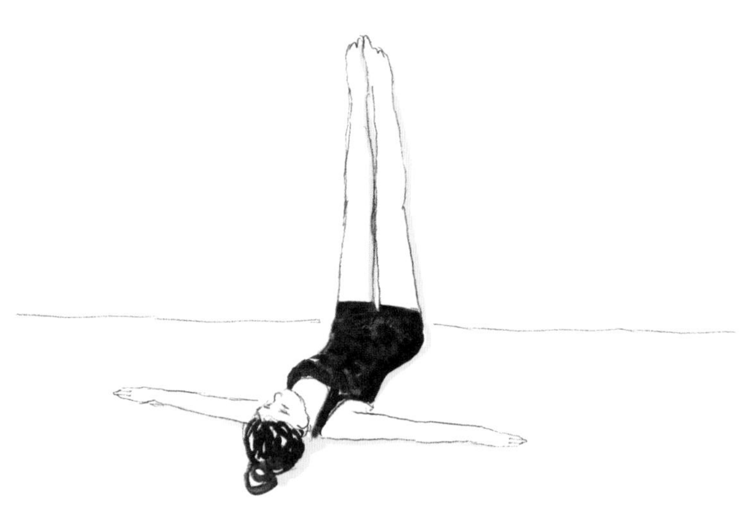

MAYBE THE WORK
ISN'T IN THE FIGURING
BUT IN THE ALLOWING.

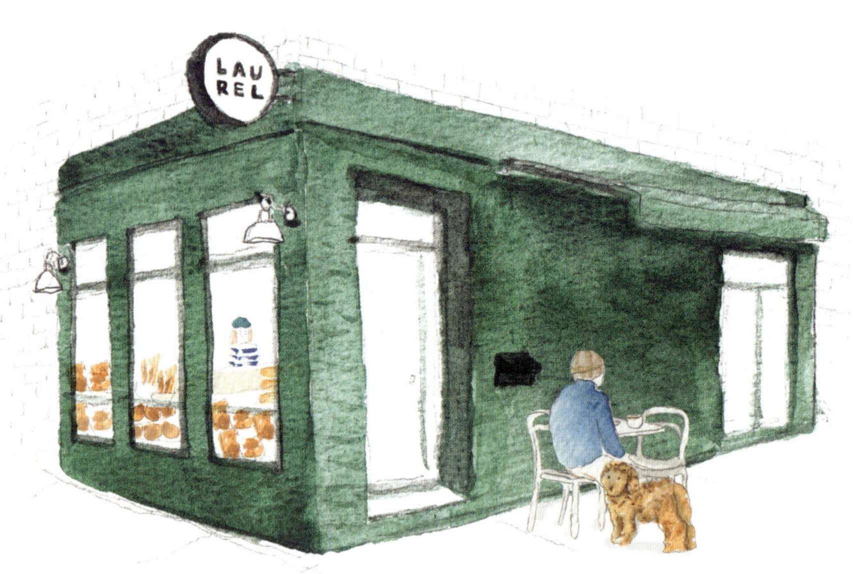
LAU
REL

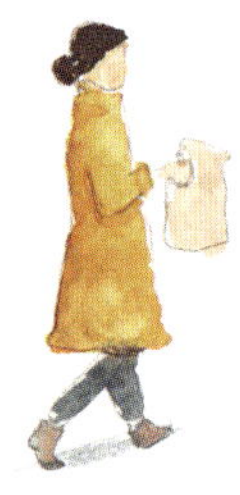

A bakery opened on Kane Street and Columbia in Brooklyn. I noticed it last week during my run to the waterfront—one of those small changes to the neighborhood landscape that catches your attention. I was drawn to the green color of the exterior and how the bakery's name, Laurel, was stacked on its circular sign.

I thought today was as good as any day to try it, so I wandered over. They had four different types of focaccia, straight out of the oven. It smelled like heaven.

A young girl worked behind the counter, and she thoughtfully packaged up my slice in butcher paper with the name of the bakery on it. While I waited, I noticed a book beside the register: *Paul Celan: Selections.*

Before I could ask about it, I thought about Coco and how she would say, "Mommy, do you have to say hello to everyone?" But, of course, she would already know the answer.

The girl told me she found the book on the street. One of her favorite things about living in New York was that people just give things away—she picked up this particular book because she had remembered someone telling her that Paul Celan was a surrealist.

Her favorite selection so far was "Corona," and her favorite lines: *It is time that the stone grew accustomed to blooming, that unrest formed a heart.*

I paid and thanked her for the words; she replied with a smile, "It was a pleasure."

As I stepped out onto the sidewalk, the city felt smaller, kinder, more connected. And I walked home, carrying more than just bread.

SOMETIMES
WE NEED A
DAY OF
NOTHING.

THE JOY OF BEING

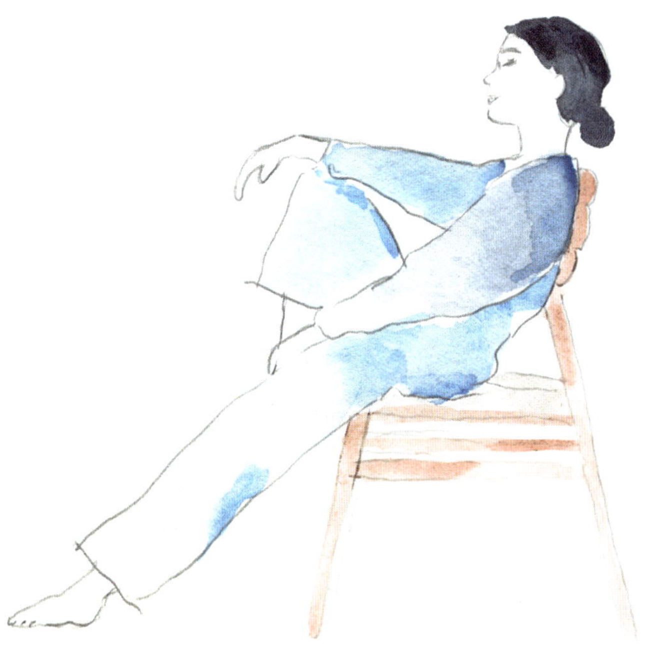

BEYOND THE OPENING

Presence has become my practice not because I'm naturally good at it but because I've experienced the quiet damage of its absence. How many conversations have I had while my mind was elsewhere? How many sunsets have I missed while scrolling through photos of other people's sunsets? The irony doesn't escape me.

My mind wanders a hundred times a day, and a hundred times I gently escort it back to what's directly in front of me. This returning itself becomes the practice, not some imagined state of perfect attention. There's a forgiveness in this approach that makes it sustainable.

What I've discovered through all this returning is that we're often running from what's actually happening right in front of us. Yet as I've learned to stay—with whatever's here, comfortable or not—I've discovered that presence doesn't just change how I see things; it changes what becomes possible.

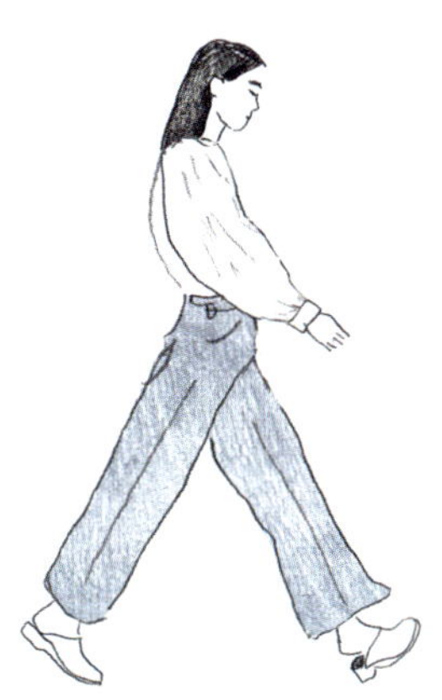

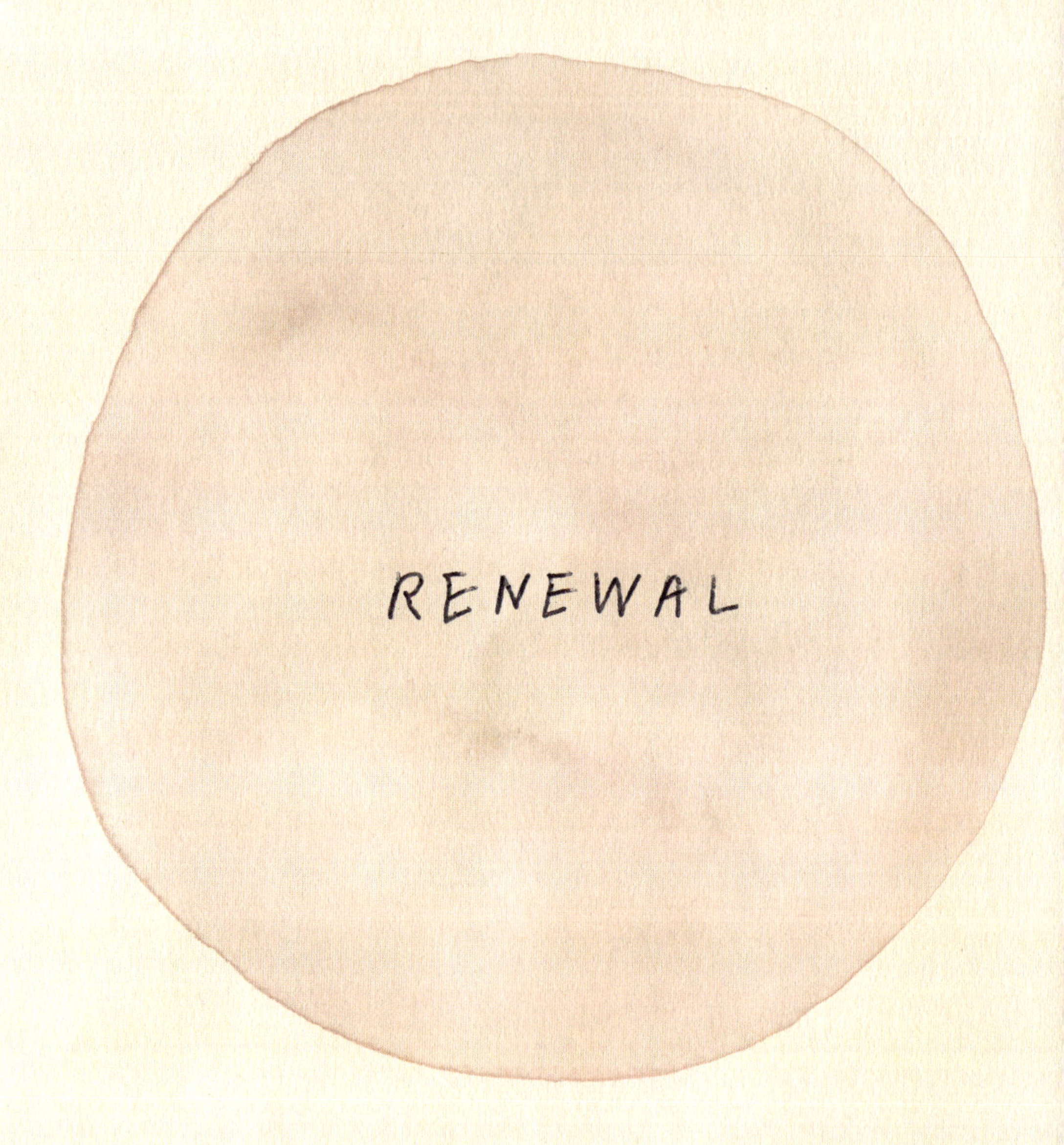
RENEWAL

PART 05: BEGIN AGAIN & AGAIN & AGAIN

RENEWAL

Sometimes we choose to begin again. Other times, life chooses for us. Whether you see it coming or it blindsides you, the invitation is the same: Loosen your grip on who you thought you had to be and see who you might become.

I've walked this path enough times to know there's no manual. Sometimes you stumble forward in the dark. Sometimes you step deliberately toward new light. What I've learned is that beginning again isn't a single moment but something that shapes a life—the willingness to keep becoming someone you've never been before.

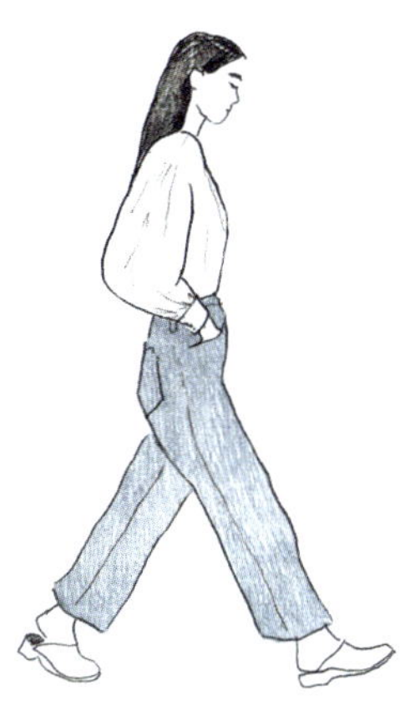

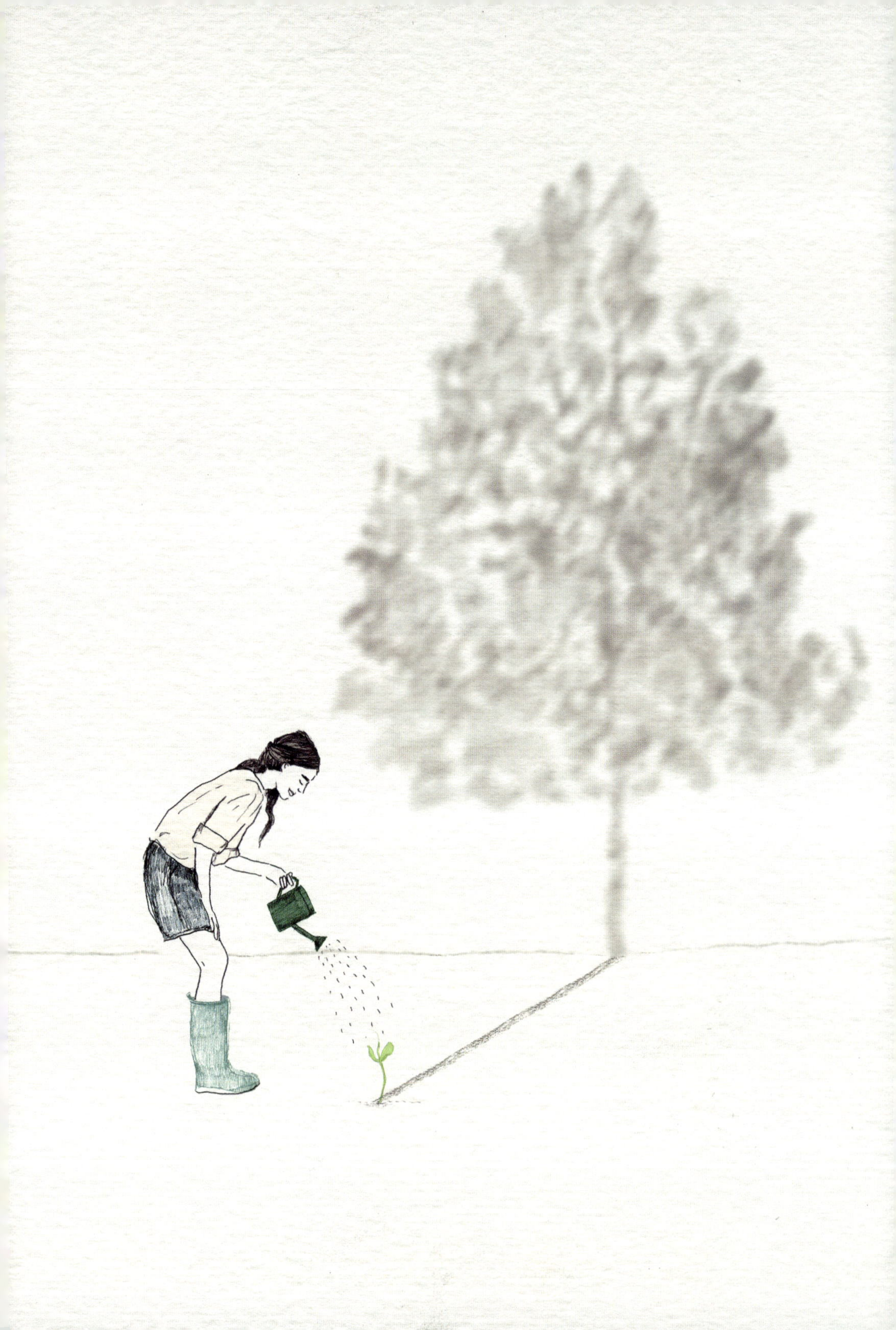

Difficult for me to accept
but the day I plant the seed
is not the day I eat the fruit

EVERYTHING
WORTH HAVING
TAKES TIME.

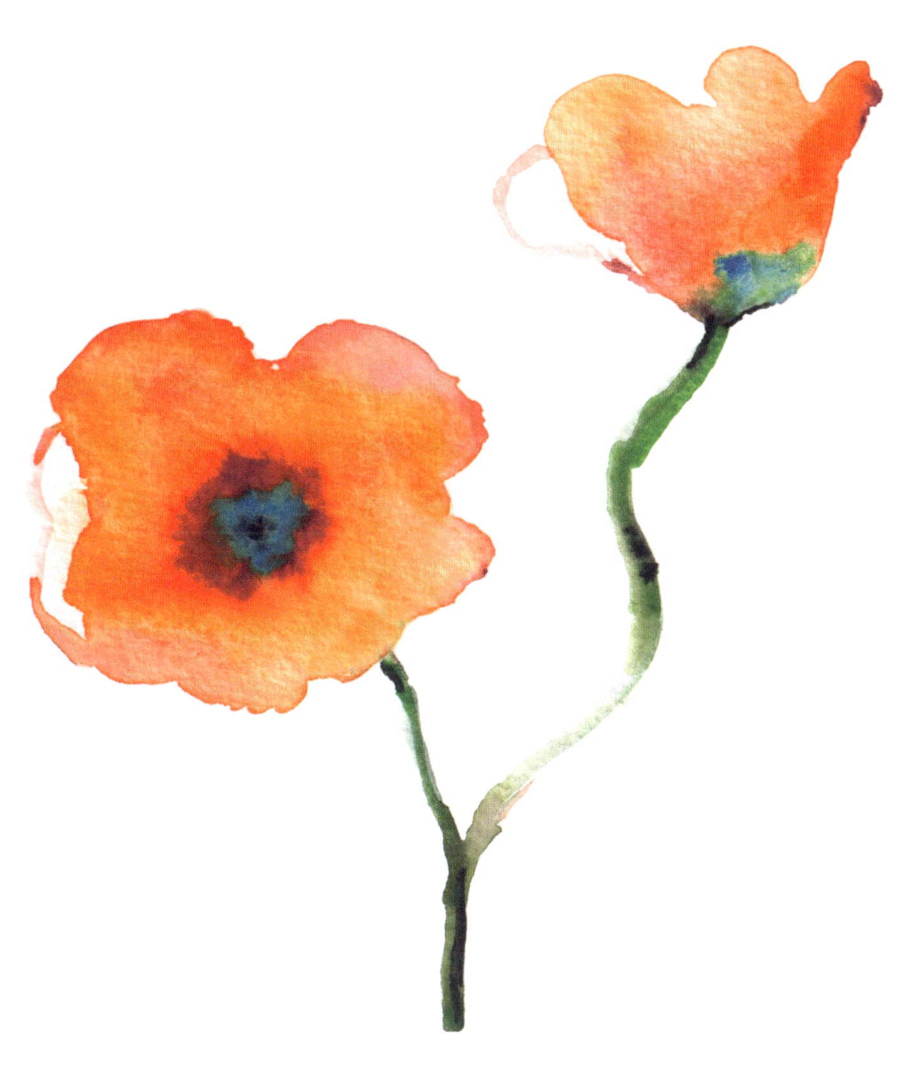

THE FLOWER DOESN'T WORRY
ABOUT BLOOMING LATE;
IT JUST OPENS WHEN
IT'S READY.

EVERYTHING
THAT COMES
INTO MY LIFE
IS A GIFT. →

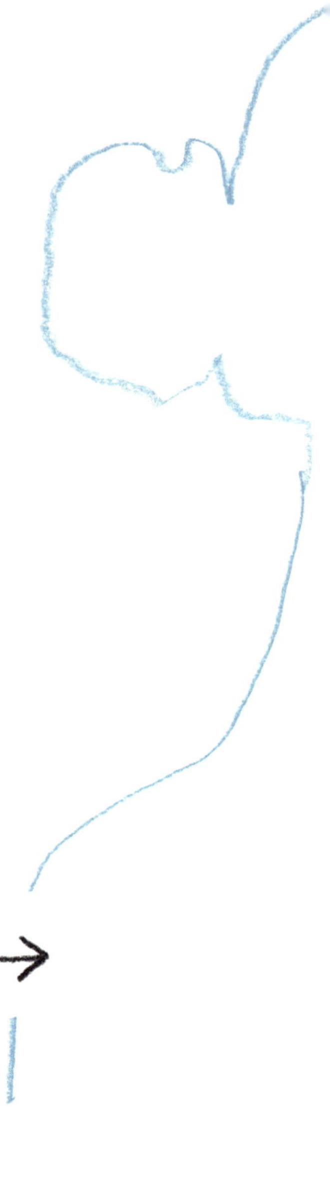

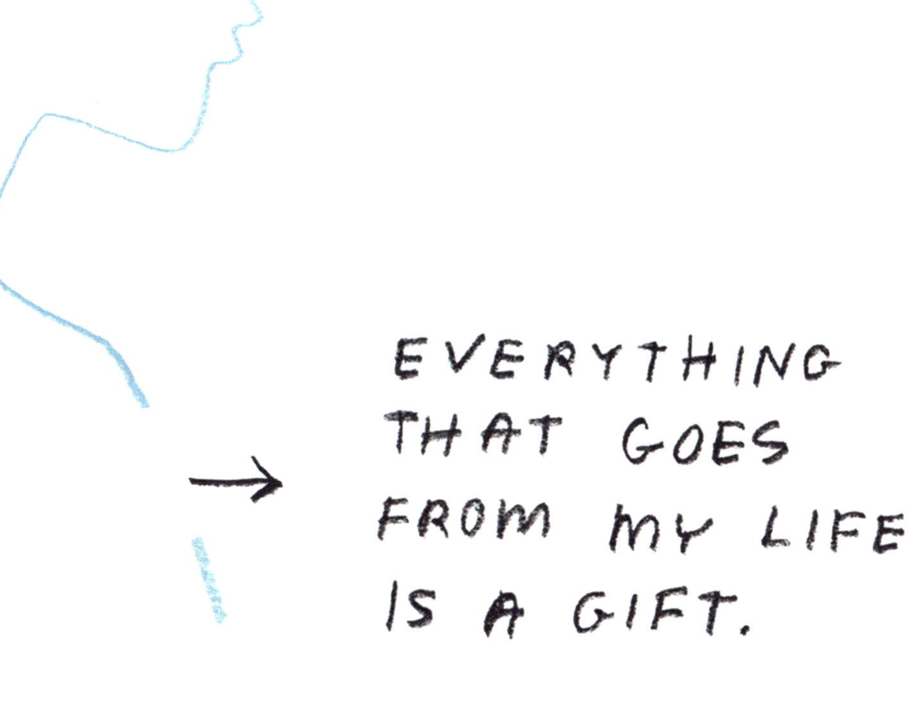
EVERYTHING
THAT GOES
FROM MY LIFE
IS A GIFT.

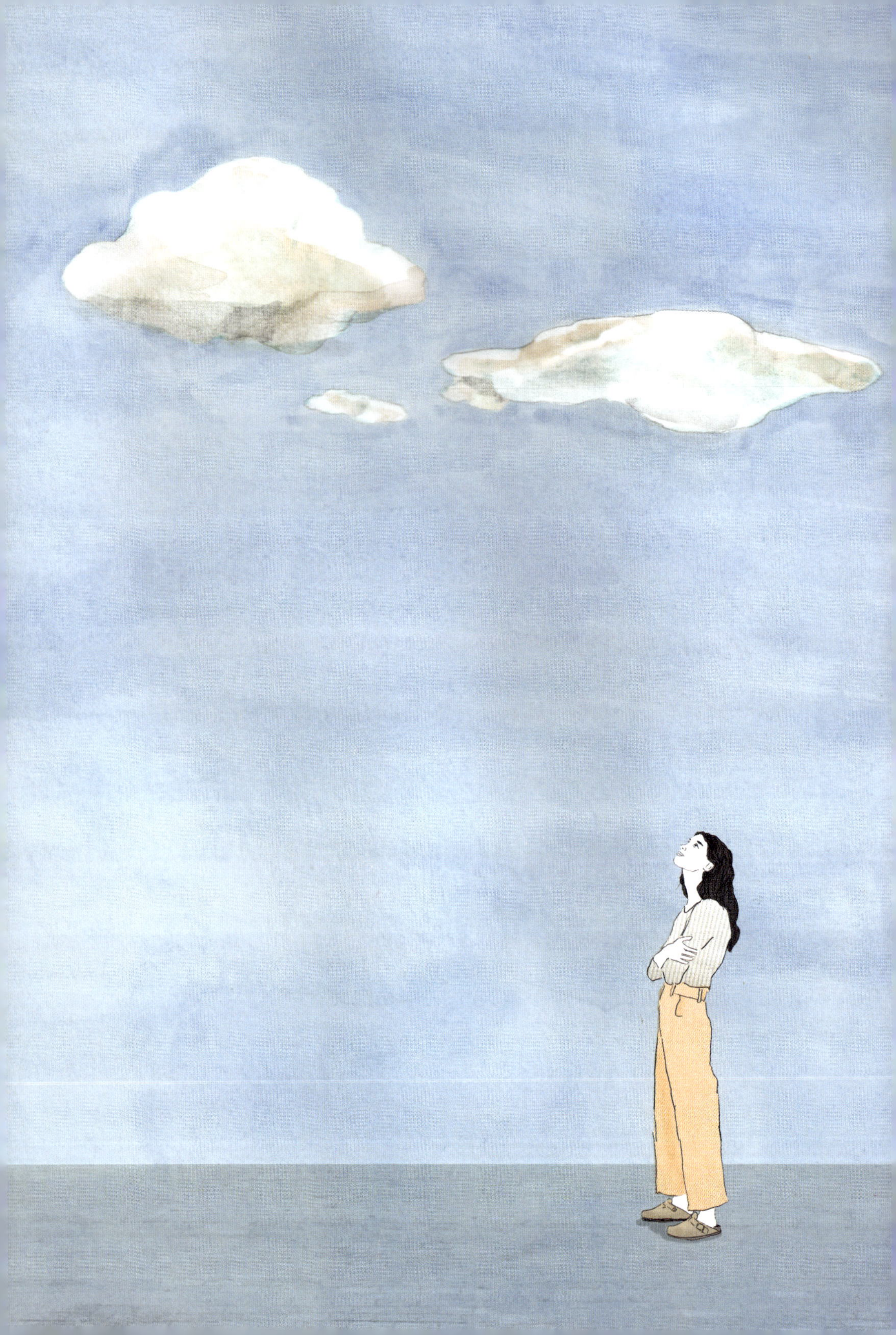

ON SELF-WORTH AND THE MYTH OF PERPETUAL MOTION

SOMETIMES YOU NEED TO REMEMBER
YOU ARE FLESH AND BONE AND FEELING.
NOT AN INBOX, NOT A TASK LIST,
NOT A MACHINE.

WHEN WAS THE LAST TIME YOU WATCHED
CLOUDS MOVE? FELT RAIN ON YOUR FACE?
LISTENED TO A SONG THE WHOLE WAY
THROUGH? THESE ARE NOT LUXURIES;
THEY ARE NECESSITIES.
PRODUCTIVITY DOESN'T LOVE YOU BACK.
STOP MEASURING YOUR WORTH IN COMPLETED
TASKS. THE UNIVERSE DOESN'T KEEP SCORE.

BREATHE. LOOK UP. STEP OUTSIDE.
BE STILL. YOUR WORTH ISN'T IN WHAT
YOU PRODUCE. IT'S IN HOW YOU EXIST.
IT'S OKAY TO BE SOFT IN A WORLD THAT
WANTS YOU HARD. YOUR HEARTBEAT IS THE
OLDEST SONG YOU'VE FORGOTTEN HOW
TO HEAR.

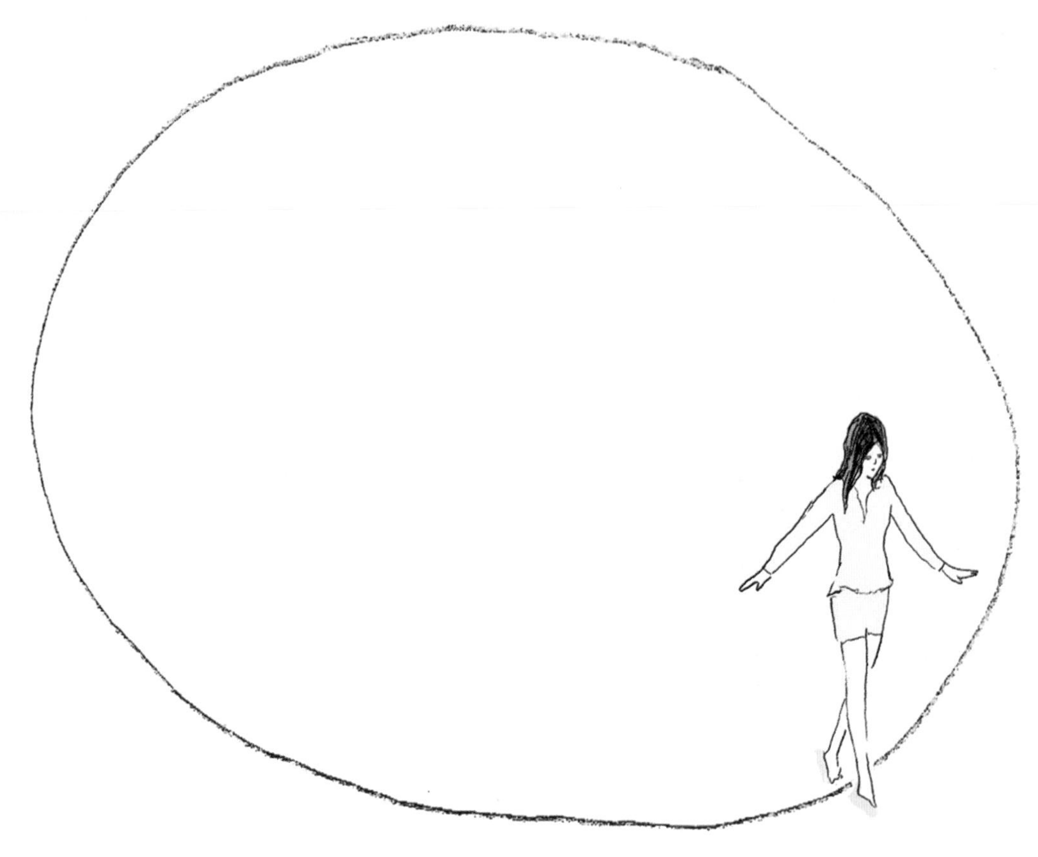

SOMETIMES GROWTH BEGINS
OUTSIDE YOUR COMFORT CIRCLE.

TAKE

THE CHANCE.

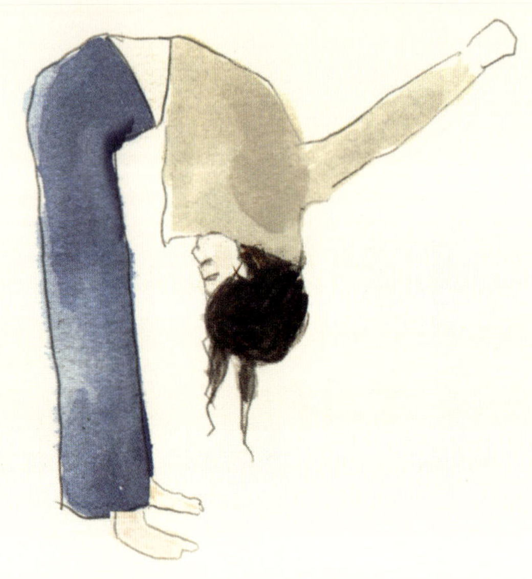

GROWTH CAN ALSO FEEL

LIKE A BREAKING POINT.

"WHAT HAPPENS WHEN YOU WAIT? THERE'S NOTHING YOU CAN DO. YOU WATCH AND ALL YOU SEE IS WHAT GOES ON THAT IS HAPPENING OF ITSELF. YOU'RE BREATHING, THE WIND IS BLOWING, THE TREES ARE WAVING, YOUR BLOOD IS CIRCULATING, YOUR NERVES ARE TINGLING. IT'S ALL GOING ON BY ITSELF. THAT'S YOU, THAT'S THE REAL YOU. BUT, THE YOU THAT GOES ON ITSELF."

— ALAN WATTS

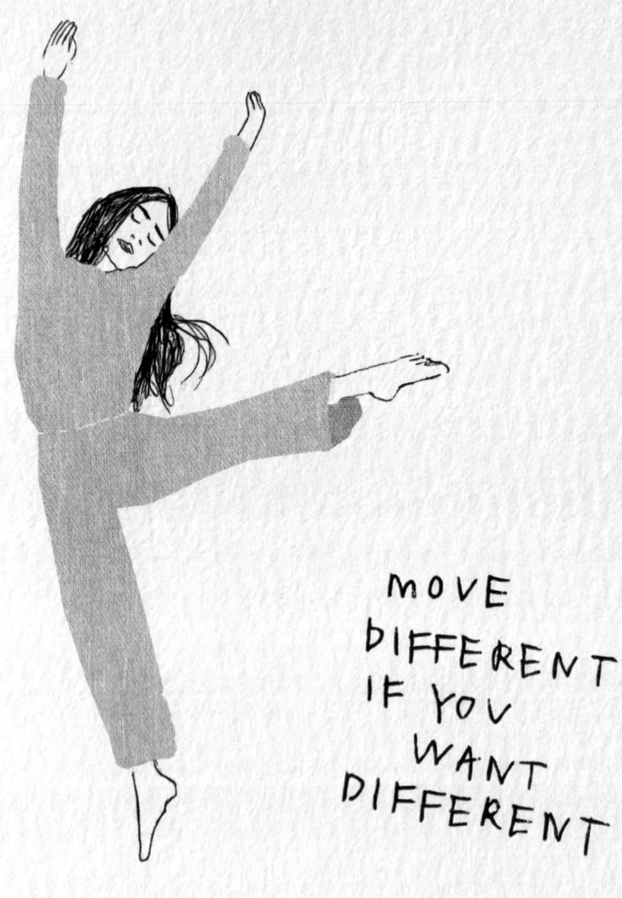
MOVE
DIFFERENT
IF YOU
WANT
DIFFERENT

COMING UNDONE

Things fall apart. This is not a metaphor.

We inherit an idea of how things "should be"—an established order passed down through generations. I learned early to cling to this order, finding comfort in its predictability. My carefully organized life, my systems, my routines—all of it a fortress against uncertainty.

But things fall out of order, again and again. The house gets messy, relationships end, coffee gets cold. My fall from order created discomfort. I resisted it, desperately trying to hold everything together.

I found myself on the kitchen floor one morning, picking up pieces of a coffee mug that had slipped from my hands. As I swept up the fragments, I thought about how often I've tried to maintain what was already broken. What I didn't understand then was that growth takes root in the breaks.

I left one small piece on the counter. A reminder that to live fully is to move between order and chaos. The unraveling isn't the problem. The unraveling is the opening.

We rise at different hours, you and I,
Strangers sharing one earth.
Some to the whir of city buses,
others to roosters' calls.
Some hands reach for coffee cups
while others fold in morning prayer.
Our paths cross and weave like threads
in an endless tapestry,
each color needed,
each pattern unique.
And when evening comes,
no matter where we are,
no matter what weights we carry,
we all have the same sky above us—
these ancient lights
that have watched over countless stories,
these stars that shine their quiet promise
on every upturned face.

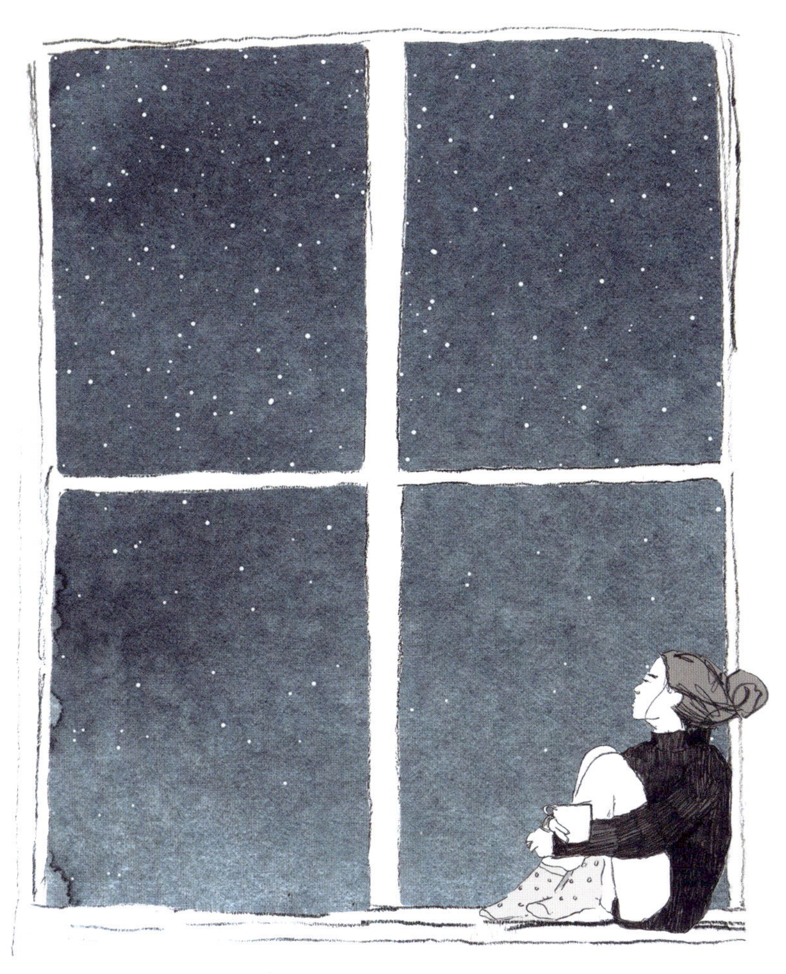

THE STARS SHINE FOR EVERYONE WHO LOOKS UP.

STAY CLOSE
TO THE ONES
THAT MAKE
YOU FEEL MORE
ALIVE.

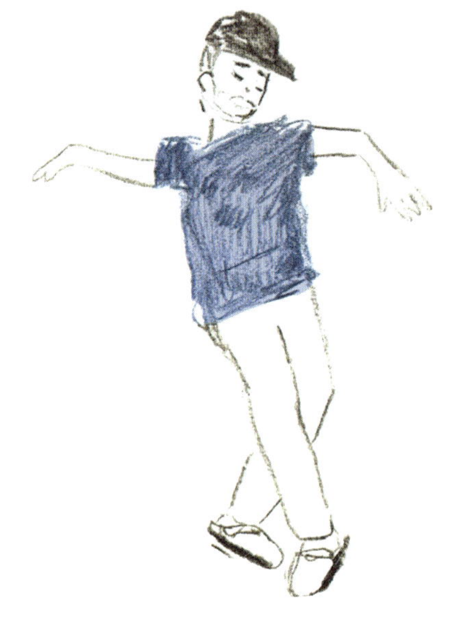

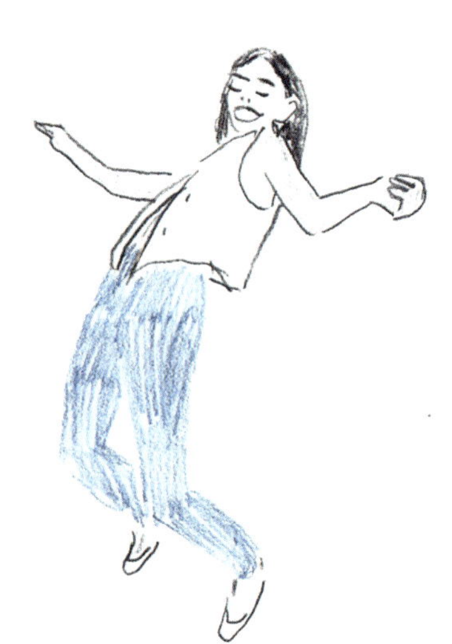

Some people are windows—
not mirrors that reflect,
but openings that let light touch
the forgotten corners of your spirit.

Seek those rare souls
who do not clip your wings
but help you understand
the very shape of flight.

In Greek mythology, Sisyphus was condemned to eternally roll a boulder up a mountain, only to watch it roll back down as he neared the summit—the ultimate picture of futile struggle.

In the space between effort and surrender, there lives a truth we often miss: The boulder isn't our burden. Our relationship with the boulder is.

We've misunderstood Sisyphus all along. His story isn't about futility—it's about finding freedom in accepting what is.

When we stop asking "Why this mountain?" and "When does this end?," something shifts. We are not punished by the repetition. We are punished by our resistance to it. Freedom isn't the absence of the boulder. Freedom is rolling it with grace.

Perhaps Albert Camus was right. We must imagine Sisyphus happy—not because his condition improved, but because he finally saw it clearly. The mountain never changes. The boulder never lightens. Yet in this understanding, everything transforms. The heaviness was never in the boulder. The heaviness was in our resistance to see today's climb.

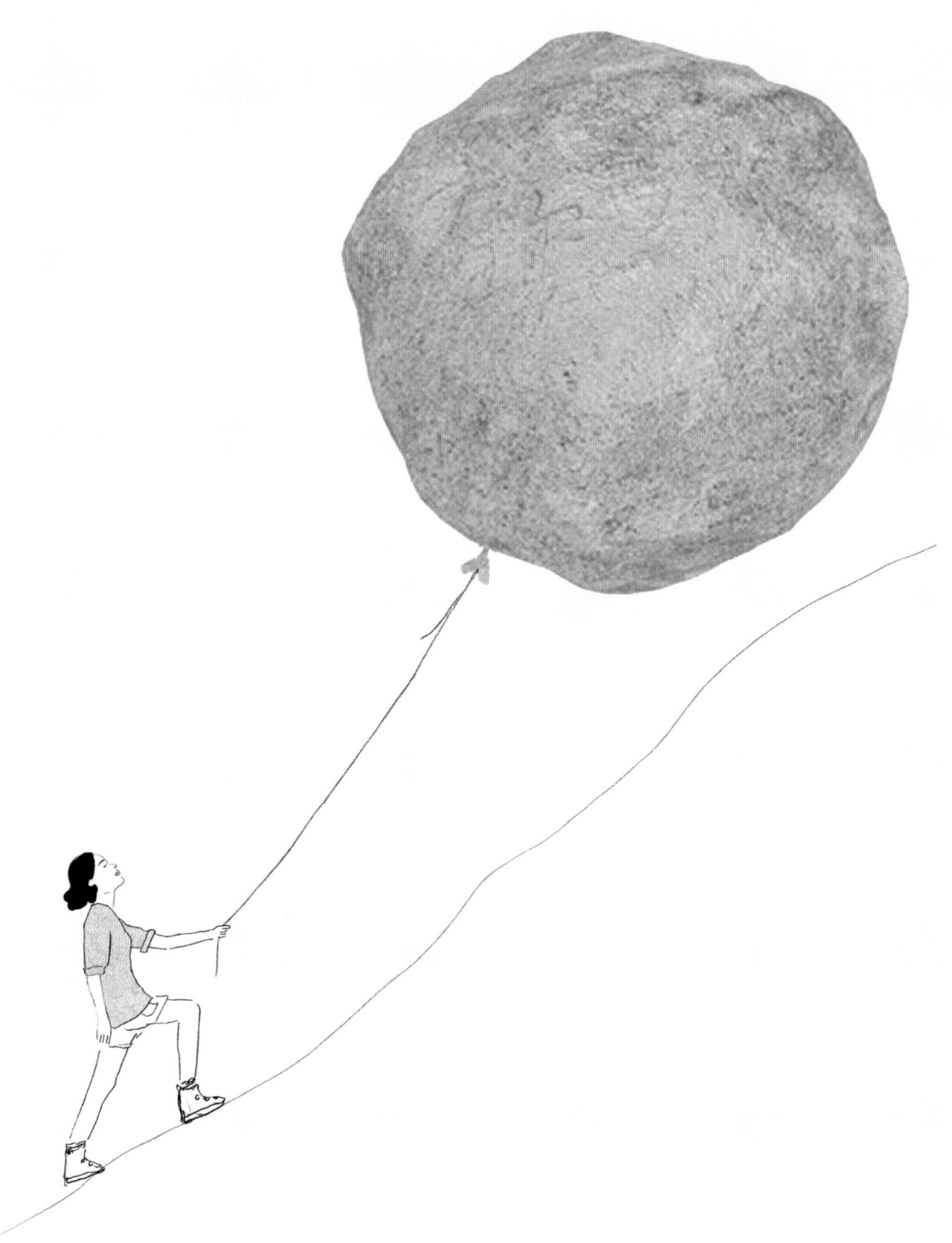

SOMEDAY WE WILL FIND
WHAT WE WANT.

OR MAYBE WE WON'T,

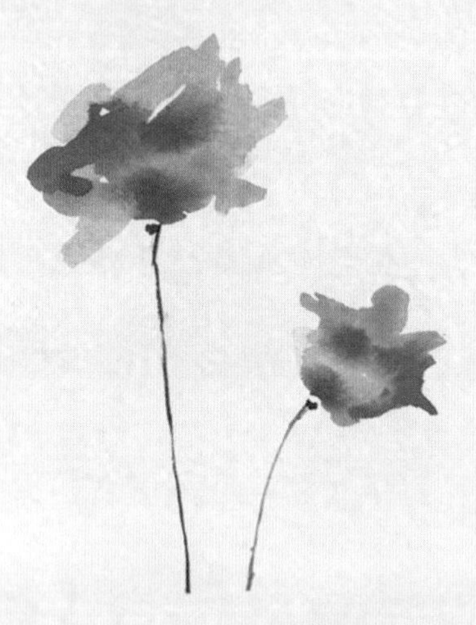

MAYBE WE'LL DISCOVER
SOMETHING MUCH
GREATER THAN THAT.

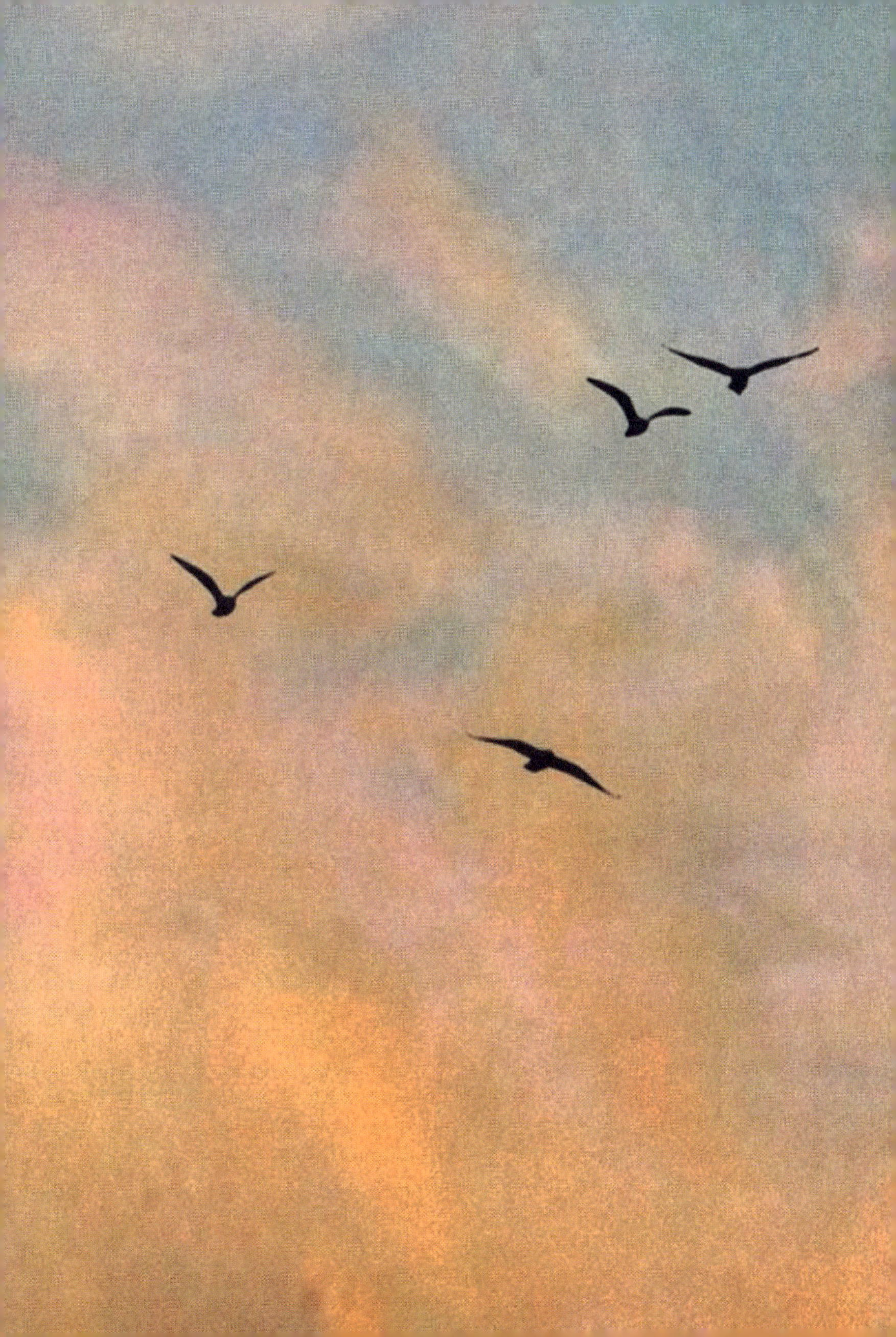

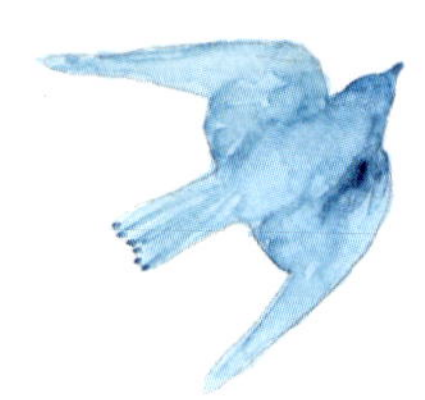

WHAT I KNOW ABOUT HOME

We arrived at our rental, a little Shaker-style cottage nestled at the top of a hill in Marin County. A small piece of wood with a white swallow painted on it hung to the right of the front door. As Coco raced in to explore, the swallow kept my attention.

Warm pine floors creaked beneath my feet as afternoon light filtered through gauze curtains. The cottage smelled of lavender and old wood—someone's careful attempt to make strangers feel welcome. On the entrance table sat a leather-bound journal, its pages filled with personal observations about the local birds.

I opened it and learned that California is home to several species of swallows. There's the tree swallow, the violet-green swallow, and the purple martin, as well as the bank, the rough-winged, the barn, and the cliff swallow. What struck me most was how these birds navigate thousands of miles each year yet return to the same place to nest each spring. A natural instinct guides them back to where they once found safety.

From the hilltop, the landscape stretched out before us. I closed the journal and stepped outside. As the sunset painted the sky, I sat on the garden swing watching Coco play in the yard. The swallow sign caught the fading light, and it seemed to glow. That's when I understood: Home isn't always a place. It can be a feeling, it can be a person, and sometimes it can be a possibility.

SKY

A PLACE TO EXIST

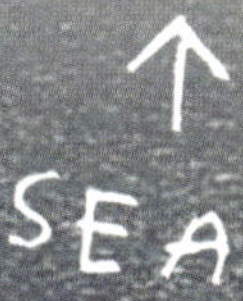

There is a place where
the sea meets the sky,
where boundaries
dissolve into something
unnamed and perfect.
I long to dwell in this
in-between space,
this gentle blur
that defies definition.
Here, in this margin
between azure depths
and endless heavens,
there is no need to
choose sides or
claim territory.
It simply exists,
as I wish to exist—
undefined,
uncategorized,
unclaimed,
free from the weight of
belonging to one world
or another.
In this liminal space,
being is enough.

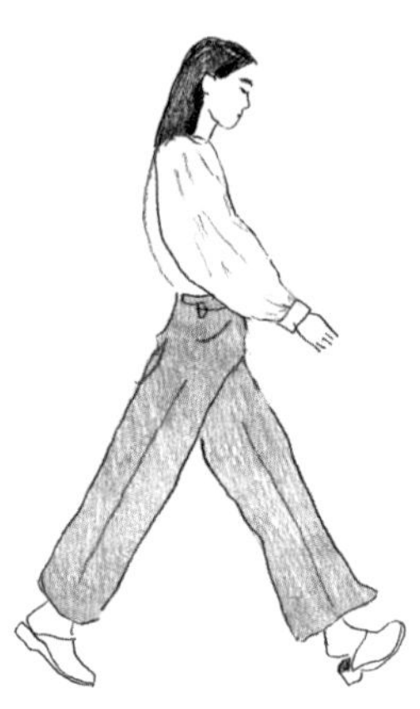

BEYOND THE RENEWAL

Throughout a life of crossroads and new beginnings, I've discovered that transformation isn't just about the moments when everything falls apart—it's also about the courage of choosing to rebuild. Each time I've stood at the edge of change, the emptiness I once feared became the space where I found my truest voice. In the spaces where my old certainties used to live, I discovered something I hadn't expected: We are not meant to remain unchanged.

The very moments that broke me open became the foundation of something more authentic—not because they destroyed me, but because they showed me how to put myself back together differently.

It requires saying "perhaps" when everything in you wants certainty, staying open when closing off seems safer. Now I understand that beginning again isn't just an act of survival but one of profound creation.

The sun rises because rising is what it knows.
The tide pulls back to gather strength for its return.
We, too, live by these rhythms—
this dance of emptying and filling,
of losing our way and finding it once more.

There is no final version of yourself waiting.
Only this beautiful spiral of transformation,
where each moment folds into the next
and loss reveals what follows.

The cycle continues, always. And we begin again.
This is not the ending. This is the becoming.

YOU HAVE NOT

MISSED OUT.

LIFE

IS

STILL

UNFOLDING.

ACKNOWLEDGMENTS

To Coco, my constant inspiration. This book is for you. May you always have the courage to begin again, the freedom to change your mind, and the quiet confidence to know you are enough.

To Fabrice, who encouraged me to be too much and held my hand while I learned how.

To my brothers, Edward, James, and Andrew, who are beginning again alongside me.

To Steve Sprinkel, poet and cofounder, with his wife, of Farmer and the Cook in Ojai, whose book *Too Late to Be in a Hurry* inspired the reflection on page 119.

To the friends and collaborators who read early drafts and reminded me why this work mattered: Dot Barad, Cara Brophy, Margaret Brown, Heather Corbett, Jill Epstein, Shoshana Gutmajer, Johannah Johnson, Tim Matusch, Andrew Olanow, Tiffany Pentz, Sasha Stern, Jane Treuhaft, Candice Waldron, and Kate Woodrow.

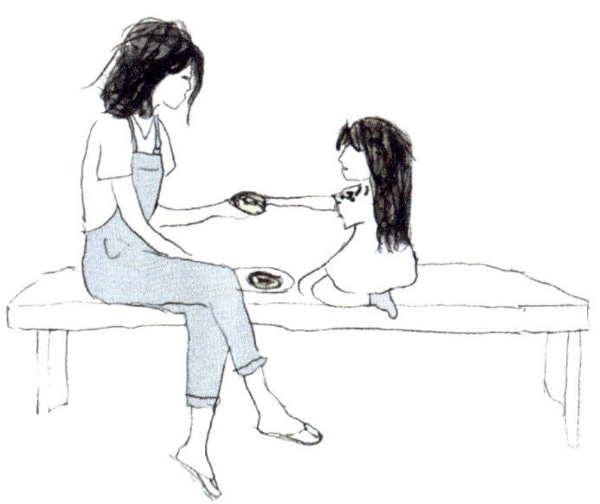

Alessandra Olanow is an illustrator and author. She lives in Brooklyn, New York, with her daughter, Coco.

Workman
Workman Publishing
Hachette Book Group, Inc.
1290 Avenue of the Americas
New York, NY 10104
workman.com

Workman is an imprint of Workman Publishing, a division of Hachette Book Group, Inc. The Workman name and logo are registered trademarks of Hachette Book Group, Inc.

Design by Alessandra Olanow and Jane Treuhaft
Jacket art and design by Alessandra Olanow

The publisher is not responsible for websites (or their content) that are not owned by the publisher.

Workman books may be purchased in bulk for business, educational, or promotional use. For information, please contact your local bookseller or the Hachette Book Group Special Markets Department at special.markets@hbgusa.com.

Library of Congress Cataloging-in-Publication Data is available

ISBN 978-1-5235-3171-4 (hardcover)

ISBN 978-1-5235-3173-8 (epub)

First Edition March 2026

Printed in China (TLF) on responsibly sourced paper.

10 9 8 7 6 5 4 3 2 1